Overcoming Rejection

The Ultimate Guide to Overcoming the Fear of Rejection

(The True Power within Yourself Overcome Rejection Shame Fear Self Esteem)

Joshua Kowal

Published By **Kate Sanders**

Joshua Kowal

All Rights Reserved

Overcoming Rejection: The Ultimate Guide to Overcoming the Fear of Rejection (The True Power within Yourself Overcome Rejection Shame Fear Self Esteem)

ISBN 978-0-9952066-8-7

No part of this guidebook shall be reproduced in any form without permission in writing from the publisher except in the case of brief quotations embodied in critical articles or reviews.

Legal & Disclaimer

The information contained in this book is not designed to replace or take the place of any form of medicine or professional medical advice. The information in this book has been provided for educational & entertainment purposes only.

The information contained in this book has been compiled from sources deemed reliable, and it is accurate to the best of the Author's knowledge; however, the Author cannot guarantee its accuracy and validity and cannot be held liable for any errors or omissions. Changes are periodically made to this book. You must consult your doctor or get professional medical advice before using any of the suggested remedies, techniques, or information in this book.

Upon using the information contained in this book, you agree to hold harmless the Author from and against any damages, costs, and expenses, including any legal fees potentially resulting from the application of any of the information provided by this guide. This disclaimer applies to any damages or injury caused by the use and application, whether directly or indirectly, of any advice or information presented, whether for breach of contract, tort, negligence, personal injury, criminal intent, or under any other cause of action.

You agree to accept all risks of using the information presented inside this book. You need to consult a professional medical practitioner in order to ensure you are both able and healthy enough to participate in this program.

Table Of Contents

Chapter 1: Classes Of Rejection

Right here are 4 number one forms of rejection, every of which comes with its personal set of intellectual worrying situations and emotional burdens. No be counted wide variety wide variety what shape of rejection you are experiencing, it's miles continuously surely beneficial to get help if you are finding it hard to cope with and take shipping of the situation. Rejection can stand up in severa situations, and any intellectual fitness results will in part depend on the ones contexts. Common types of rejection include:

Family Rejection

This can take the form of abuse, abandonment, forget, or the withholding of love and affection. Parental rejection is the most not unusual of the own family rejection. An individual is in all likelihood to be stricken by this form of rejection for the rest of their lives, and it is able to have bad consequences.

Parental rejection is the maximum frequent form of this shape of rejection; however it can moreover rise up among siblings. It may also moreover include many kinds of emotional abuse, in addition to forget, abandonment, and a lack of care and love. People who experience this form of emotional rejection may go through the effects for the relaxation in their lifestyles.

Social Rejection

This form of rejection can arise to all and sundry at any age and frequently begins in early infancy. Bullying and alienation at artwork or at faculty are examples of social rejection, even though it is able to have an impact on any social organisation. People who stay "out of doors the norm" for their society or who oppose the recognition quo can be more likely to revel in social rejection.

People normally enjoy this kind of rejection quite early in lifestyles. It can encompass the whole lot starting from bullying of numerous sorts to highschool exclusion. However, it can have an effect on human beings of all ages, at the side of adults and individuals of different social organizations. People who have a tendency to venture the recognition quo are extra susceptible to this form of rejection.

Why Does Social Rejection Occur?

Every human has a deep want to fit in. Some argue that that is because of the reality human beings don't have claws or fangs, making us as an alternative vulnerable to predators; very last in a fixed helped us stay on. Because of this, those those who have been more centered closer to agencies survived. As a stop end result, all contemporary people are very organisation-orientated.

Whether or no longer this evolutionary clarification is correct, we do apprehend that having a experience of network, social involvement, and relational willpower is crucial for our health, pride, or maybe survival. The maximum fine thing for our health and well-being can also in reality be social connection. Our enjoy of belonging consists of components and they may be:

It consists of mechanically having tremendous social interactions.

It offers a sturdy framework primarily based definitely mostly on shared problem.

Being a part of a network now not first rate makes us enjoy like we belong, but it moreover validates our critical ideals and offers us a sense of self confidence. Overall, this makes social approval specifically critical to us and reasons us to sense exquisite soreness even because it takes vicinity.

Relationship Rejection

People may additionally encounter rejection in the course of courting or in a devoted courting. Examples embody withholding affection or closeness from a partner, refusing to percentage an experience or occasion with them, or treating them like a passing acquaintance. A man or woman's selection to surrender a relationship can every so often make the alternative partner revel in unwelcome.

Romantic connections are commonly the only context for this shape of rejection. It might be some aspect from your associate refusing to proportion a personal second with you to the relationship truly completing. This shape of rejection commonly effects in rapid, extreme emotional distress. In the ones conditions, lengthy training instructions is probably quite beneficial.

Romantic Rejection

This can get up even as someone requests a date however one is grew to emerge as down. Although this could from time to time be known as sexual rejection, a person who has been rejected romantically won't usually be inquisitive about having a sexual connection.

Any form of rejection may be painful, however on the same time because it comes from a trusted loved one, it may have a specifically terrible impact on one's revel in of self confidence and self-self guarantee. Therapy can help human beings heal from wounds that could cease end result from being rejected through a loved one, however it could additionally help human beings learn how to receive rejection that happens in every day life, which encompass being rejected with the useful resource of way of a capacity romantic associate, being rejected all through a task are looking for, or being rejected at the same time as making use of to college.

The 'Friend Zone' and Romantic Rejection

Romantic rejection can be extremely difficult, specifically for folks that want an extended-term self-discipline. When a love relationship ends or you are rejected with the beneficial aid of a companion, you could revel in extreme grief that lasts for weeks, months, or perhaps years. Long after a romantic courting has ended, rejection can alternate how a person sees their existence and themselves.

The concept of the "friend vicinity" has received recognition currently. A individual who says they had been "located within the pal region" is generally relating to the rejection of amorous advances made on the character they had been interested by. Typically, this takes area in virtually in reality one in every of two conditions:

When someone tries up to now a person who handiest wants to pursue friendship along side him or her.

Although all people can use the word "being pal zoned" to give an explanation for a situation of rejection, the word is maximum frequently utilized by and with the useful resource of grownup adult men who've been rejected with the beneficial aid of women, and is visible through many as complex.

While many people might be able to be given that the individual whom they may be drawn to might not experience the equal way, others have to enjoy furious or disenchanted. Some human beings need to suppose that thru being type to someone, they advantage the opportunity thus far that man or woman and win their affection. Others could probably expect that maintaining a friendship with a person they will be interested in will offer them the threat to expand romantic emotions for them and the urge to are looking for a romantic courting with them.

These principles have the capability to decorate the ideals that romantic love is most important to friendship, that humans (commonly ladies and men) cannot be friends with out seeking to have intercourse, and that everybody desires to have sex (getting rid of the research of folks who are aromantic or asexual).

The phrase "guy and female" is not typically utilized in that enjoy. When used on this manner, it can offer a lift to the notion that women, or everyone who rejects each distinctive, can't be held responsible for their very own points of interest or dating options and might not apprehend what they need.

This way that after a lady rejects someone, she won't clearly suggest it or also can respond otherwise in the destiny. The idea that human beings are heterosexual until they explicitly indicate otherwise or that heterosexuality is the "ordinary" sexual orientation is a few different motive why the "friend quarter" may be stated to make contributions to heterosexist mind.

Typically, the time period "guy and lady" does now not have that connotation. The concept that girls, or all and sundry who rejects each exclusive, can't be held chargeable for their very very own points of hobby or relationship options and won't apprehend what they want can be strengthened at the same time as carried out on this way. This shows that a girl won't imply it at the same time as she rejects a person or that she would probable act in every other manner inside the future. Another manner that the "pal location" can be argued to contribute to heterosexist perspectives is the perception that people are heterosexual besides they expressly state otherwise or that heterosexuality is the "normal" sexual orientation.

Chapter 2: Formats Of Rejection

No marriage will continuously be sunshine and butterflies. Because relationships are complex, verbal exchange problems can get up. Your massive accomplice and also you might not continuously agree on everything. You have in all likelihood encountered a few sort of rejection on your marriage sooner or later. You may probably experience rejection in lots of special methods, including both bodily and emotionally.

Rejection is inevitable in life, however the way wherein your partner rejects you may display lots about your marriage. Does your accomplice make concessions or simply dismiss you? Whether or not the relationship is healthful may be decided thru how they respond in your "no" and the way you decide to deal with it.

How precisely need to you respond at the same time as the person you adore rejects you? The most wellknown kinds of rejection are indexed under, on the facet of some recommendations on how to take care of the feeling of being exceeded over.

Silent Rejection

It can be thoroughly provoking while your companion ignores you once you pour your whole coronary heart and soul into your marriage. Because it makes you revel in so terrible approximately yourself, being omitted may be as painful as receiving a flat "no". You can also grow to be indignant and irritated due to the fact you recall your partner does now not want to be spherical you. Rejection can be surprisingly difficult to conquer for humans who have terrible conceitedness and can purpose further setbacks. You and your companion should have a few excessive conversations if this shape of rejection takes vicinity frequently thinking about it's miles in no manner suitable in a marriage. If it is not efficiently addressed, it will cause your marriage to fail.

Careless Rejection

Having your companion assist you to understand "No" outright is the toughest kind of rejection The final trouble you need to do is offer your associate the effect that you are extraordinarily unkind and unpleasant. Because you do get maintain of a response, it is higher than being surely overlooked, but that doesn't make it any loads less painful. Taking a step back from your emotions and comparing the problem logically is the high-quality method to gct higher from an outright rejection. Why do you're taking delivery of as genuine with your companion is performing so adversarial? Do you and your accomplice need to speak about some factor else proper now to your dating? It's crucial to try to keep away from beginning a brawl right after this cold rejection. Instead, calm your self earlier than trying to offer an cause of why this wounded you.

Consensual Rejection

Sometimes at the same time as your companion rejects you, they provide a compromise to try to lessen the effect. Being given the danger to attempt another time inside the destiny makes this shape of rejection the right to deal with. It serves as a reminder that your accomplice is not refusing your request out of spite for you; instead, there can be a motive within the back of it that probable has not anything to do with you. It will depend upon your choice a way to respond to this sort of rejection how topics enlarge. If you still be furious, your accomplice can also additionally accept as true with that you do now not cost their feelings or care about the motives they'll be rejecting you.

Both you and your companion could have possibilities to beautify if you make a decision to virtually be given the endorsed compromise and speak about it with courtesy.

Courteous Rejection

A rejection, even one this is in a polite manner phrased, can severely have an impact in your familiar performance. No depend how kindly your companion emerge as about the denial, it but motives you to pause and endure in mind your options. It aches! Additionally, this extends beyond your partner's rejection. According to a University of Michigan Medical School have a study, the thoughts responds to social rejection in a manner much like the manner it responds to bodily harm.

They did take a look at, however, that the greater you emerge as acquainted with receiving well mannered rejection, the heaps a whole lot much less painful it's far to cope with it. You will eventually come to be extra familiar with rejection as you open up to your companion, to the point that it no longer negatively influences you. Naturally, this only applies if your companion behaves in a type, peaceful way.

Your vanity can go through if you are rejected, and it could make you revel in unwelcome for your marriage. See if there are a few other techniques to your partner to explicit their sentiments approximately deciding on to say "no" to you without making you sense unwanted. Even in case you and your associate don't usually need to agree on everything, a loss of regular communication can quick derail your courting.

THE PHASES OF REJECTION

How normally can a person be rejected? Understanding rejection is useful earlier than you could take delivery of your emotions. In phrases of emotions, accepting rejection is a method, just like grieving a loss. You will development thru the stages as you work via your emotions, subsequently getting past the disappointment, self-doubt, and anger you are presently feeling to transport on and locate serenity.

Depending on you and the condition, you may spend diverse amounts of time coping with rejection. Some might possibly skip more rapidly than others. It's critical to exercising self-compassion. There isn't any great charge for overcoming rejection.

The 5 stages of rejection are indexed beneath:

1.   Refusal

Your preliminary response whilst mastering someone has rejected you'll be surprise. There want to be an mistakes. You ought to probably enjoy that some thing isn't always quite right due to the truth you deserve this person's recognize and admiration.

2.   Anger

That's denial, and after identifying that your rejection wasn't the quit end result of a miscommunication, you may start to feel disillusioned. You can turn out to be enraged once you discover the person rejecting you is not seeing their errors in judgment.

It may be tempting to lash out on the person who rejected you in the intervening time. Not in any respect. In the surrender, yelling at them will clearly make you sense worse about yourself. Take some deep breaths and attempt to loosen up. You must attempt to control your wrath in this example and permit calmer heads succeed.

3.   Negotiating

You'll reach a 2nd wherein you start to take into account that the person who will let you down did so due to an wrong assumption or a lack of knowledge. You'll trust that if you may genuinely communicate with them, you may have an effect on them.

If you permit it, this diploma want to fast come to be some element frightful for the other man or woman. You need to provide the individual that rejected you some room. For the sake of your potential future dating, must you each determine to pursue it, you should graciously take transport of their preference. They are not required to offer you a purpose for their rejection.

4.   Depression

A tangled knot of emotions accompanies rejection. You're unhappy, ashamed, puzzled, damage, and angry on pinnacle of being disappointed and outraged. Your self confidence may be in query, and your self belief has suffered. These are all legitimate reactions to rejection that might set off depressive symptoms and signs.

You need to place yourself-care habitual on excessive alert right now. Make your self cushty with friends, slight candles, or take a bubble bathtub. The entire aspect that makes you experience cushty. As quick as you experience comfortable, start probing your feelings to determine which ones are inflicting your despair and increase a approach to deal with them. Reminding your self of all the motives you are a extremely good man or woman and of all the individuals who care about and cherish you'll be all that is important.

5.   Recognition

It's time to analyze the situation now that your emotions have stabilized and you're feeling greater like your former, self-confident self. Perhaps the purpose you've got been rejected became that you were not an excellent in shape or that there were one-of-a-kind extenuating situations.

You may additionally additionally moreover understand a mistake you committed and understand it as a training 2nd. It's furthermore probably that you'll in no way apprehend all that came about in detail. That's great too. Whatever occurred, you grew and found from the experience. Because you presently understand the method, you may be better geared up to understand your feelings the subsequent time you're rejected.

How Does It Feel to Be Rejected?

According to some surprising studies, social rejection definitely resembles physical pain in the manner it feels. Both the sensory and emotional elements of pain are activated within the corresponding mind areas via this.

The pain reaction will boom intensive with the degree of rejection. Particularly, the thoughts produced every emotional and bodily ache reactions whilst human beings idea approximately a contemporary-day romantic courting breakup. Because of this, while human beings claim that social rejection hurts, they definitely endorse it!

Why Being Rejected Stings:

It hurts to be rejected thru a pal, a potential romantic associate, or a chairman. The distress you revel in is actual; there may be a purpose it is called rejection trauma. The same part of your thoughts is engaged at the same time as you are processing this statistics, whether or now not you are hurting from a finger lessen or rejection harm.

Rejection influences us emotionally similarly to physical because of the truth we crave recognition and a sense of belonging. Humans are social beings, and our strength to engage with others has advanced over the years. People who speedy assimilated into the tribe have been much more likely to live on and procreate beginning even as human beings lived collectively as hunter-gatherer corporations.

People who struggled to form sturdy relationships with others were more likely to be rejected or labeled as outcasts. The call for to be protected developed right into a natural requirement over time The times surrounding rejection battle along side your evolutionary urge, which leads to worry and self-doubt.

If you sense the ones emotions even as a person rejects your presence, you are not inclined or emotionally risky. It is organic. You don't have any control over how you may enjoy while you are for my part disillusioned; what you could manage is how you'll react to the situation that is inflicting these sentiments.

Chapter 3: Reasons For Rejection

Rejection is painful. There genuinely isn't any getting round that. Most people choice a experience of network and connection, specifically with the ones they care about. No recollect if it is for a profession, a romantic courting, or a friendship, it is ugly to enjoy unwelcome and unwanted thru the ones people.

Also, the pain has a as an possibility sharp vicinity. In reality, rejection reasons the equal factors of the thoughts to spark off as bodily ache does. Hence, it is straightforward to look why such a lot of humans worry rejection. If you have got got passed via rejection as soon as or more, you are probably to endure in thoughts how painful it have become and fear about it taking vicinity all all over again.

However, being fearful of being rejected can prevent you from taking possibilities and aiming excessive. Fortunately, with a touch attempt, it is really possible to change this mind-set. Here are some guidelines to help you get going via rejection. Keep in thoughts that everyone research it. Fear of rejection is a totally common emotion, and rejection is a considerably commonplace revel in.

Most people encounter rejection as a minimum some times of their life for each large and insignificant reasons, together with:

A student not receiving an invitation to a chum's birthday party

A buddy ignoring a message about setting together

Someone getting rejected for a date

A lengthy-time period companion quitting for every other

Some elements inside the again of some of these rejections can be:

Wrong software program software or resume

Inappropriate profile/wrong set of abilties

Not in shape

Physically now not worthy for any unique employment position

Passionate however fed up

Limited Experience

Ineffective Communication

Lack of Confidence

Insufficient Recommendations

Excessive Salary Expectations

From the attitude of the candidate, rejection is not a lousy thing but as an alternative a workout to research from and get better for upcoming opportunities. It need to be normal in a wholesome manner that employment strategies encompass choice and rejection. Even even though it in no way feels pleasant at the same time as topics do no longer skip as planned, now not all of lifestyles's situations pan out as deliberate. You may additionally need to experience masses a lot much less scared of rejection if you remind yourself that it's far handiest a ordinary part of life and anybody will revel in it in the long run.

What Brings about Rejection in Relationship?

This is one problem that has remained unresolved for a while. If you have got ever skilled rejection in a relationship, you can be left wondering precisely what you probable did to earn that treatment. Yet, good day! Understanding exactly what outcomes in rejection in relationships is the first step in preventing this.

Perhaps your accomplice isn't always ready yet.

One of the precept reasons for rejection in relationships is that this. Someone who isn't but prepared for the duties of a dating with you could war and in the long run reject you. If you're the simplest who is unprepared, the same element can take vicinity. You can be the handiest to keep away from interacting at the side of your accomplice.

Another element that might result in courting rejection is stress.

When you are with a person who is sporting spherical quite some weight immediately, they could find it difficult to emotionally connect to you. They may also then retreat into their shell as a stop result, principal you to bear in mind which you have been rejected.

When Do We Experience Rejection?

Although rejection regularly takes place on cause—this is, while a person rejects you—it does now not constantly. The degree to which we're touchy to rejection and can be given as real with that someone is rejecting us while they are now not genuinely differs amongst us. For example, although someone is not searching out to reject us, their loss of smile or amusement at our jokes can be taken as rejection.

Women can also typically experience rejection greater strongly than grownup adult males. This might be due to the fact that women generally have a tendency to prioritize social ties extra than adult men do. As a end end result, women may additionally enjoy rejection in relationships with extra ferocity.

How Do We React When We're Rejected?

Rejection should have some pretty unsightly effects as it breaks down social relationships and reasons us to experience a big form of poor feelings.

First, it is able to impair cognitive task performance. All folks have awful thoughts and feelings weighing on our minds.

Second, it makes human beings extra aggressive and can possibly bring about violence.

Third, it would inspire greater self-focused conduct.

Fourth, it is able to impair our functionality to control our impulses—yup, we truly ate the whole bathtub of ice cream due to the fact we have been feeling rejected!

CONSCIOUSNESS TO REJECTION

How Does Rejection Sensitivity Work?

We range in how we recognize and respond to rejection, as have become already cited. While a number of us would possibly see our pal's choice not to ask us to lunch as a rejection, others might also moreover provide the excuse that they clearly forgot or failed to anticipate our hobby. And the actual purpose of our friend can be very precise.

Rejection-sensitive human beings are folks who commonly have a tendency to be conscious on the same time as they'll be rejected in even the tiniest approaches—or even don't forget that they may be being rejected whilst they're now not. Therefore, the tendency to "anxiously expect, truly understand, and overreact to rejection" is assessed as rejection sensitivity.

Where Does Sensitivity to Rejection Emanate from?

Many pupils contend that repeated rejections as children, frequently from a figure parent, purpose the improvement of rejection sensitivity. If our dad and mom or special adults treated us harshly, unfavorably, or negatively at the same time as we have been young, we may additionally moreover make bigger to count on the equal remedy in interpersonal connections in the gift and the destiny. We ought to accumulate fears of abandonment, shame, and betrayal that reason us to appearance rejection where it does now not exist or to study it even as others may not.

What Are the Effects of Rejection Sensitivity on Relationships?

Being rejected may moreover make you more sensitive to rejection, that may be a splendidly everyday and logical response. But simply due to the fact some thing makes revel in does no longer suggest it's miles properly for you. In truth, rejection sensitivity can also by the usage of risk stimulate the rejection-related reviews we seeking out to keep away from.

It should probably make us experience constantly insecure in our relationships and make us overreact even as we feel our partner has rejected us. Relationships can be tested via our competitive, resentful, or dominating behavior introduced on through the usage of our sentiments of rejection. This is certainly one instance of approaches changing how we understand rejection and the way we react to it may help us form healthful relationships.

What Does Rejection Sensitivity Dysphoria Mean?

An immoderate form of rejection sensitivity known as rejection sensitive dysphoria can from time to time be visible in people with autism or hobby deficit disorder. These people also can have trouble focusing their interest and controlling their feelings. It can be tougher to preserve outstanding reactions to real or hypothetical rejection as a prevent end result.

Fear of Being Rejected

The sensation of rejection is idea to have developed as a survival mechanism to warn early those who should likely lose their place of their network. A man or woman became in all likelihood to change any unstable conduct after experiencing painful rejection from specific tribe contributors at the way to prevent in addition rejection or ostracism from the organization. The chance of survival turned into better for those who have been capable of prevent more rejection, while the chance of survival changed into lower for folks who did now not find out rejection to be mainly painful and might not have changed the problematic conduct. In this way, it is viable that people have superior to discover rejection painful.

These days, masses of humans isolate themselves or keep away from making connections with others out of a worry of being grew to come to be away. Chronic emotions of loneliness and disappointment can quit end result from someone taking flight from others out of worry of or sensitivity to rejection. It isn't a identified analysis, no matter the reality that rejection sensitivity can co-arise with quite a few intellectual health conditions, which include social tension, avoidant character, and borderline character.

Many people with hobby-deficit hyperactivity infection (ADHD) revel in rejection sensitivity regularly. Some human beings with ADHD may also furthermore have rejection sensitivity dysphoria due to the truth they worry rejection so often. Self-complaint, social anxiety, and intense depression following a perceived rejection are a number of the acquainted symptoms of rejection touchy dysphoria in humans with ADHD.

PERSONALITY IMPACTS OF REJECTION

What Has Being Rejected Done to A Person?

People who revel in rejection also can come to trust that they're no longer desired, official, or traditional, which can be extraordinarily hurtful. Most humans will stumble upon rejection at the least as quick as in their lives. A pressured-out determine may also make a little one revel in rejected momentarily, even as a stern or nasty professor also can make a pupil feel rejected.

When someone rejects you, their preliminary reaction is emotional misery. While some varieties of rejection can be resolved quick, which incorporates being rejected with the aid of way of impolite strangers, extraordinary sorts of rejection may also have more excessive repercussions. Continuous or prolonged rejection may want to have profound and enduring psychological impacts, which could consist of:

Trauma: Rejection that lasts for a long term or that reasons excessive sensations can cause trauma and function horrible intellectual consequences. Children who sense frequently rejected with the resource in their parents, as an example, may war academically and socially with their classmates. Some humans undergo a chronic dread of rejection, regularly due to numerous annoying rejection research subsequently of infancy.

Long-time period rejection and intense rejection can each have a sizable psychological impact on a person. For instance, a little one who memories repeated emotional rejection from their dad and mom may additionally furthermore struggle in college or have problem building relationships later in lifestyles due to the fact they'll be terrified of rejection.

Depression: Teenage women who bear rejection are more likely to increase melancholy; though, people who come upon rejection might also moreover moreover enjoy despair. Bullying, this is in truth a mixture of exclusion and rejection, can also have some of unfavorable influences, together with depression, stress, eating disorders, and self-harming behaviors.

There are times wherein rejection and despair are associated. Even if this handiest takes vicinity within the maximum intense situations, the mere risk that rejection can bring about despair necessitates coping with the emotional results of rejection.

Response to Pain: It has been discovered thru studies that the mind reacts to social pain in a manner that is similar to the way it reacts to bodily pain. Researchers have decided that social ache, or rejection, activates the equal brain pathways as bodily ache does. When a person suffers social ache, just like while physical ache is skilled, receptor systems in the brain also release herbal painkillers (opioids).

Rejection can result in bodily pain for a person, at the same time as mental and emotional suffering is more regularly the consequences. When you undergo physical ache, the same regions of your thoughts which is probably activated at the same time as you go through emotional suffering also are active.

Stress and Anxiety: Rejection can also exacerbate pre-present day symptoms and signs and symptoms and symptoms like strain and tension or motive their onset. Similar to how the ones and one-of-a-kind intellectual fitness issues can heighten rejection feelings.

Rejection can exacerbate the emotions of strain and anxiety if you already warfare with those troubles. Being rejected also can result in anxiety and strain, therefore it is critical to be aware of this.

Abuse: According to a take a look at, male members' involvement in abusive interpersonal relationships turned into greater common after they had formerly skilled better degrees of parental rejection. Posttraumatic pressure illness signs and deficiencies inside the processing of social statistics have moreover been connected.

Although rejection is probably painful, it is in no way an first rate concept to apply bodily or mental abuse or violence towards a few different character to vent your frustration. For instance, a take a look at found that feeling rejected may additionally encourage violence or anger in the course of that business enterprise. People who experience rejection can learn how to deal with perceived or actual rejection and increase social talents that can permit them to have interaction with others greater without difficulty with the useful aid of a sympathetic therapist.

Why Does Rejection Hurt So Much?

Being purposefully driven far from a person you care approximately is what is meant through rejection. Whether it's far a partner, a member of your own family, a coworker, or a pal, rejection can still go away you feeling damage and distressed.

In a few relationships, long intervals of emotional manipulation can be logically determined through the usage of emotional rejection. However, now not all people may be sincere about their motives for rejecting you, and it is not unusual on the way to be ignorant of the underlying problem.

This is why rejection can be quite hard, especially in case you are given no justification. Other times, the intensity of the broken connection makes the struggling worse. No rely what form of rejection you are coping with, there is an extremely good hazard it's going to depart you feeling disillusioned, have a negative impact to your conceitedness, and in a few situations, even make you depressed.

Chapter 4: 15 Red Flags Of Rejection In Relationships

Do you enjoy as even though you are being ignored? Here are 15 signs and symptoms of rejection in romantic relationships.

1.   They in no manner move again your calls or texts.

Can you bear in thoughts how matters become whilst your dating have become absolutely getting started They usually once more your calls and texts inner a few seconds, giving the impact that they continuously had their phones with them.

But one of the telltale caution signs of rejection in a dating is abrupt silence. They now see your texts but in no manner reply. They in no manner select up your calls and in no way name you decrease back.

2.   They have drifted apart

It from time to time feels as even though you're with a stranger even at the same time as you're within the same room as them.

Just now, strategic conversation has become rendered out of date. Even no matter the truth which you changed into once close friends, you slightly talk to every other anymore and love each particular's employer.

3.   You appear to be fighting nonstop proper now.

You experience as despite the fact that you're unable to percent the identical issue of view all over again. However, the motive you cannot seem to prevent preventing is generally due to the fact they appear like going out of their way to criticize the whole thing you do.

Now that their expectancies have skyrocketed, it seems not possible to pleasure them because there can be no danger that they will make any concessions for you.

4.   They're continuously busy.

While each dating associate have to have their private lifestyles, the significance of spending time together as a couple can't be overstated. Spending incredible time together with your associate complements the extremely good of your courting, in accordance to analyze. But how can this stand up on the identical time as you are with a accomplice who becomes relatively busy?

When you want them, they in no manner come thru. They begin working bizarre hours and journeying some distance from home all of a surprising. These are the numerous most obvious warning signs of rejection in a relationship.

5.   They claimed they were no longer organized for dedication.

The first time you listen this, you may discover yourself rolling your eyes (inside the useless choice that they will get over it short). However, inside the occasion that they have got a tendency to shove some detail to your face, you can want to pay more hobby.

Even if they may be announcing it with a huge sneer on their face, a supposed partner who maintains insisting they're not organized for a willpower is typically looking for to keep away from your interest and your offers of willpower.

6.   They may not supply your courting a call.

Have you ever encountered a person who desires all the blessings couples are entitled to however is in no manner willing to really commit? They prolonged for the love and closeness that encompass being dealt with like a large unique, however they're in no way prepared to go all the way in.

When you ask them to present an cause of your connection, they shift the problem and refuse to famend which you are nothing more than "friends" with them. It will become difficult the extra you press them to take action.

7.   They begin to re-listing themselves available on the market

When someone (or girl, for that don't forget) rejects you, one of the maximum obvious symptoms is they start to positioned themselves decrease lower returned to be had. When they first met you, they deactivated their courting net web page debts. But do not be amazed in case you locate that they've revived some of those dating sites and are virtually lively there another time. Your partner may be ready to stop the connection within the occasion that they suddenly start showing hobby in dating different human beings.

8.   They start flirting lots.

It is one aspect to have a partner who acts flirtatious a bit bit after ingesting too much at a celebration. However, you could want to reevaluate your dating if your associate usually fancies every other eligible individual they stumble upon without regard for your feelings.

You might probably encounter certain parents on your life who honestly adore the concept of flirting. Even if they will be in extreme relationships, they'll nonetheless flirt every now and then. But within the event that they recognize and love their relationships, they'll restrain themselves from doing this.

However, in case your associate maintains to flirt with each person they may be capable of, no matter the way you experience, it could be a sign that they're making ready to prevent the connection.

nine. They've recommended you from a depended on deliver.

All the caution symptoms we've got were given blanketed to date are simple to push aside. However, that a close buddy or family member of your associate would possibly fast make contributions is one of the most telling signs of rejection in a dating. This can be the cease end result of some thing your companion stated to them in advance. Even even though you want to no longer see this due to the fact the very last signal, be cautious not to ignore it every.

10.   They do not offer you with any big plans with you.

When a person consists of you in their future plans, it is one of the most effective ways to tell in the event that they charge you and need to move critical. They speak to you approximately all of the desires they have got for the future and unique a preference with a purpose to be part of it.

On the alternative hand, in case your partner couldn't make any employer arrangements with you, it's miles a sign that you can start to revel in rejected within the courting swiftly. On the opposite hand, in case you are normally their fallback and by no means their pinnacle priority, that may be a warning flag for you.

eleven.   You have not but gotten to recognize their closest own family and buddies.

If your accomplice is reluctant to can help you meet their circle of relatives and closest pals, this is one sign that a letdown may be on the horizon. Meeting their own family is normally regarded as a massive step toward dedication. However, in case you are relationship a person who typically exhibits a justification to prevent you from meeting their loved ones, you would possibly need to pause.

Nevertheless, take interest to what they've got to say. Has this meeting ever been said? No? Those is probably symptoms of relationship rejection.

12.   When you try to introduce them on your own family, they withdraw.

Every romantic courting is inspired by using manner of circle of relatives dynamics, and in case your circle of relatives is not supportive, your courting may additionally moreover moreover undergo. It is one problem on your partner to save you you from seeing their circle of relatives and friends. However, you could need to reconsider in the event that they constantly withdraw whilst you try and introduce them to oldsters which can be closest to you.

How do they reply while you thing out the assembly and introducing your own family? When you invite them to meet your closest friends, do they hesitate? This may be the case considering they want to bypass on you within the destiny.

13.   Suddenly, your sexual lifestyles is over.

Your previous sexual life was top notch. With them, physical closeness become explosive because of the fact you shared a sturdy emotional bond. At that issue, it modified into difficult to maintain your hands wreck away one another, and also you eagerly predicted your passionate encounters. Something seems to have long long long gone wrong for the time being.

The couple's sexual life dying sincerely is one of the telltale warning symptoms of rejection in a courting. Most of the time, this drop-in sexual activity cannot be associated with a selected purpose, along aspect a fitness trouble, growing responsibility due to having youngsters, or stress.

Most frequently, the couple's weakening emotional bond is what motives this drop-in sexual hobby. However, if you approach them about having intercourse, you can even get the bloodless shoulder.

14.   They keep to push you away

Your lover might also moreover start unexpectedly pushing you away as one indication that they will be laid low with rejection tension When you try to connect to them (such as you as quick as did), they'll reject you. When you try to confide in them, they may get antagonistic and leave. When you try to start a polite communique with them, they also can try and harm you verbally.

Pushing you away is one indication that your partner is probably preparing to reject you. When you try and acquire out to them for an proof, despite the fact that, they won't have any compelling justification for his or her behavior.

15.   You can not rely on them for guide any extra

Earlier, you can name them whenever you desired some thing. They constantly added on their promise that will help you, as you knew they might. But nowadays, the narrative has modified. You find out that they will be no longer the partner you as quickly as knew whilst you try and reach out to them for solace and an answer. You can attain a point in that you no longer turn to them for assist or comfort through the years.

Rest assured that a few trouble may also additionally furthermore have lengthy past incorrect if you cannot rely upon your partner for physical or emotional manual.

Chapter 5: Dealing With Rejection

Life is about pursuing goals. And even as we do, there may be constantly a chance of being rejected. Rejection Has an Impact on Us, Big or Small. All

Rejection want no longer include number one setbacks like being rejected from your pinnacle university preference, failing to make the squad, or now not receiving a promenade invitation. Feelings of rejection can also give up end result from normal sports, which include at the same time as your joke wasn't received properly, no person concept to save you a seat at the lunch desk, or whilst the character you're in reality into chats to anyone but you.

Whether or now not we're rejection touchy, we might also continuously gain from analyzing more healthful techniques to address our rejection. This might also reduce the bodily and emotional suffering that contains rejection. These strategies may be carried out to cope with social rejection from friends or circle of relatives, rejection in love relationships, and rejection at artwork. The contrary of feeling normal is feeling rejected. But being rejected could now not mean that a person is not preferred, favored, or valuable (and we're capable of all revel in rejection at instances). It genuinely manner that as quick as, in a single circumstance, with one character, matters didn't turn out as planned.

Being rejected hurts. But keeping off it in truth isn't possible. In fact, you do not need to: People who develop overly fearful of rejection also can hesitate to pursue their desires. They might not experience rejection, however they may be in truth high great to skip up the possibilities they do not pursue.

Strategies for Handling Rejection

Here are a few techniques for handling rejection:

1.   Accept that rejection is an inevitable part of existence

Not everything works out as planned. Additionally, rejection can bring about development. It shows that you're going past your consolation zone and taking opportunities. You're performing some element wrong in case your existence is without rejection.

2. Express your unhappiness in writing.

Writing about your feelings and any capacity repercussions after receiving rejection also can assist you technique your sentiments greater fast and drift beyond them, in accordance to analyze. Check out the ones articles on every day journaling and journaling thoughts if you need extra advice on writing therapeutically.

3. Develop the potential to just accept rejection.

Accepting rejection (in location of analyzing or describing it) want to make the unsightly emotional reactions go away quicker. Acceptance does now not continuously come obviously, of course. Remembering that popularity is not much like resignation might be useful while education splendor. Tolerating a awful state of affairs or performing like a "doormat" aren't examples of beauty. Simply said, recognition consists of recognizing and accepting who you're, your mind, and your feelings. Afterward, you could take crucial movement from a position of popularity.

Denying rejection is the worst reaction to it. It may be extra hard to get over the damage and sadness the longer you fool your self into thinking it would now not rely. You've been upset. Recognize it, along side all of the different emotions that accompany the harm of rejection.

4.   Manage your feelings

Make an try to apprehend your emotions and efficiently manage them. Avoid getting irritated and venting your frustration on the other person. Rejection does damage, however that does not provide you with license to damage one-of-a-type humans.

5.   Be compassionate with your self

When going via rejection, it's far suitable to retreat for a while. You need time to attend to your self and get lower returned on a honest emotional keel. Don't criticize or second-wager your self. Be kind and do not forget that you could have a look at new matters even as you are prepared.

6.   Pay hobby to the satisfactory

Although rejection may be in particular painful, some research suggests that it is able to without a doubt make it less difficult to get proper of entry to satisfied feelings. This also can propose that proper now, nice emotion-based completely emotion manipulate techniques can be extra a achievement.

7.   Keep fit

Keep an eye fixed constant on your physical and emotional well being. It's easy to grow to be slowed down in dissatisfaction to the aspect in which you allow subjects slide. Your thoughts is focused and you are prevented from dwelling on rejection through exercising or gaining knowledge of a current day talent. Instead of wallowing in the beyond, you remember the prevailing.

Getting help from a expert is vital if your depressed state persists for extra than weeks irrespective of your notable efforts. Contacting a highbrow health expert isn't always a few issue to be afraid of. You can analyze coping mechanisms and strategies from a counselor or psychotherapist that will help you circulate on from destructive mind and emotions of rejection without looking lower once more.

8.   Don't permit rejection outline who you are

It makes enjoy that your initial reaction to rejection may be to ask what is incorrect with you. When social rejection occurs, a shy person may react with the useful resource of turning into even more of an introvert.

Though you might be the sweetest fruit at the tree, keep in mind that now not anybody like peaches. Continue being actual to yourself, and you will draw individuals who charge the whole lot you want to offer.

nine.   Learn from the stumble upon

Although rejection hurts, obsessing to your mistakes might not assist you skip beyond them. Make an try to view the scenario objectively. Can you draw any conclusions from this? If you've got been rejected for a activity possibility, ask for fine grievance that will help you figure out the way to enhance your CV.

Were there any caution signs and symptoms in the relationship that failed to exercising that you omitted along the manner? Make use of that facts as a foundation to help you get prepared the subsequent time you decide to place yourself to be had.

10.   Consider doing away with yourself emotionally from the rejection.

Imagine being a fly on the wall or a stranger on the street as you experience rejection whilst you emotionally distance your self. The unpleasant feelings may work greater unexpectedly if you endure in thoughts your situation from the attitude of a person else.

eleven.   Use acetaminophen to reduce rejection pain

A absolutely fascinating observe discovered that taking Tylenol (acetaminophen) after being rejected truely decreased the wounded sentiments. Therefore, a Tylenol may be useful in case you're feeling determined to lessen the brink of rejection. However, you can do with out it as it could have aspect consequences.

12.   Recognize your emotions.

It hurts however wherein the rejection got here from. Even whilst different humans might in all likelihood suppose it is now not a massive problem and assist you to recognize to transport on, the sorrow can also linger, particularly in case you take area to be greater sensitive to rejection. Other uneasy emotions, such awkwardness and embarrassment, may also moreover accompany rejection. Only you have were given the capacity to particular your emotions to others. It's vital to certainly receive your sentiments of rejection in advance than you can begin to address them. If you lie to your self and say you do not care in case you are wounded whilst in fact you do, you lose the danger to stand and efficiently cope with this fear.

13.   Seek out the instructional possibilities

Even even as it may now not appear that manner earlier than everything, rejection can gift chances for non-public boom. Imagine which you have a look at for a way that you really need and which you had a wonderful interview, but you aren't hired. You ought to to begin with be devastated with the resource of the usage of this. Nevertheless, after giving your résumé every other test, you can recognize it'd now not damage to examine a number of your skills and pick out out up a few new software program software usage.

After some months, you'll apprehend that the today's records has given you get admission to to higher-paying jobs for that you were in advance than unqualified. It can be less tough to move after what you need and much less painful if you fail if you reframe your tension as an opportunity for development. If some issue does not exercising, attempt reminding your self, "This won't education session, however if it doesn't, I'll have a large enjoy and recognize more than I did."

Reviewing what you in reality want in a mate will assist you triumph over rejection anxieties in phrases of romantic relationships. It can also additionally furthermore make you to be at the right music to locating a in form proper away.

14.   Convince your self of your charge

When you take rejection too in my opinion, it could be really scary. For instance, you might be concerned that you bored a date partner or that they did not find out you appealing sufficient within the occasion that they all of sudden give up responding on your texts after a few dates. However, wishes mismatching is frequently the reason of rejection.

Ghosting is by no means a first rate method, but a few people in truth do not apprehend a manner to speak properly or trust that being honest via way of expressing, "You're exquisite and lovable, however I did not quite enjoy it," will make you enjoy upset while, in reality, you may revel in it.

You can also consider which you are genuinely deserving of affection via the usage of increasing your self-worth and self belief, so that you could make you experience an entire lot much less hesitant to preserve looking for it.

Try:

identifying five techniques you stay out your
personal requirements;

writing a paragraph describing 3 times whilst
you are most thrilled of your self;

and reminding your self of the benefits you
can convey to a courting.

15.   Maintain your feel of mind-set

You may think severa worst-case situations in
case you are more sensitive to rejection and
spend severa time stressful about it. Let's say
you had been no longer traditional into the
graduate software of your choice. You may
also start to worry that you may be rejected
with the aid of way of every software you
carried out to and will need to try again the
subsequent yr.

But you then virtually definately begin to
worry that you may be grew to turn out to be
down another time the subsequent 365 days,
which will make it now not feasible on the
way to land the pastime you need and
improve your career, if you want to make it

now not feasible a good way to ever emerge as financially strong sufficient to recognise your dream of domestic possession and beginning a circle of relatives, and so on.

Catastrophizing is a form of terrible highbrow loop this is commonly unfounded. Create a few actionable backup plans for your self or come up with arguments to dispel a number of your biggest worries.

16.   Identify   what   rejection   actually frightens you.

You can address that unique tension through investigating what's certainly the use of your worry of rejection. Perhaps you are concerned about being rejected romantically due to the truth you do no longer want to be on my own. Realizing this can additionally inspire you to prioritize making lasting friendships, that could shield you from loneliness. Or perhaps you are worried approximately getting have grow to be down through using feasible employment because of the reality you lack a backup plan and experience insecure approximately your financial state of affairs. If you do no longer right away land the mission you're seeking out, outlining some capacity strategies can be beneficial.

17.   Confront your phobia

It's proper that you could no longer face rejection in case you do now not placed yourself accessible. But you may additionally likely fail to satisfy your desires. You have a risk to achieve success in case you move after what you preference. It's feasible that you may be rejected, however it is also viable which you can not.

A "fear hierarchy," or a listing of steps related for your worry of rejection, may be created. Each step can then be tackled one after the alternative. Exposure treatment consists of this. While you may do this in your private, a therapist moreover permit you to in developing a list and on foot via it.

Someone who's frightened of being rejected romantically may also start with the beneficial useful resource of creating a courting profile without any plans to use it right away. After then, they may be able to begin corresponding without any plans to meet in person. Just ensure to allow mother and father realize that you are not but attempting to find to satisfy in case you select to do that.

18.   Reject self-defeating thoughts

After receiving rejection, it is easy to boom a addiction of self-complaint. It's viable that allows you to utter phrases like "I knew I'd mess that up," "I did not prepare sufficient," "I talked an excessive amount of," or "I'm so stupid."

Nevertheless, this simplest serves to confirm your notion that you had been to be blamed for the rejection, although it can now not had been your fault the least bit. A self-enjoyable prophecy can emanate if you count on someone will reject you because of the reality you are not real enough, that may stress you to behave in fear.

Although it would now not usually art work that way, excessive first-rate thinking also will let you see topics in a clearer manner. You're much more likely to consider in your capability to gain your goals even as you guide and encourage your self. If topics don't exercise consultation, try and be compassionate with yourself via telling yourself what you may inform a cherished one in a comparable state of affairs.

19.   Rely for your community of supporters

It can help you to experience more wanted in case you spend time with individuals who care approximately you. A sturdy assist tool gives comfort in case your efforts fail and encouragement at the same time as you attempt to perform your desires. The prospect of rejection may additionally look lots less terrifying even as you understand that your family will guide you regardless of what takes place. You can also exercise exposing yourself to rejection conditions with trusted pals in case you're worried about it.

20.   Consult a professional

Fear of rejection may additionally furthermore have lengthy-lasting affects, inclusive of retaining you from pursuing great possibilities at your place of job or college. Even if you may surmount your anxieties of rejection for your non-public, getting professional assistance can occasionally be very useful. If your worry of rejection:

motives you to experience anxiety or panic attacks, it might be time to think about seeing a therapist.

prevents you from doing belongings you preference to do

upsets your ordinary existence

What to Do

Less rejection hurts us as we turn out to be extra adept at managing it. How can then you definately definately growth that capability for adjustment?

These are a few thoughts:

Be honest.

Utilizing each your thoughts and emotions are key components of powerful rejection coping.

Starting with emotions, inform your self whether or not or not or no longer you have been rejected. Do no longer try and downplay your struggling or act as although it isn't always there. Consider how extremely good it is to feel the way you do, given your situations, in vicinity of feeling like "I want to not enjoy this manner." Take note of how robust your feelings are. Did this rejection genuinely make you indignant? Or pleasant a hint bit? You can cry in case you need to; crying is a healthy technique to get feelings out.

Next, describe the way you revel in. As an example: "I'm very unhappy that I wasn't decided on for the college play. I without a doubt have worked so tough and preferred it so badly. Because my pals succeeded and I did no longer, I feel excluded. Tell someone else what came about and the way you experience approximately it in case you want to. Choose a supportive and receptive man or woman.

For reasons, telling a person else can be beneficial and they may be:

Knowing that someone empathizes on the facet of your state of affairs and the manner you experience can be comforting.

You are forced to unique your feelings verbally.

Acknowledging feelings let you get thru hard feelings, whether you want to talk approximately them with someone else or hold them to yourself.

Be Upbeat

It's very clean to come to be fed on with the aid of manner of using a awful emotion like rejection at the identical time as you are going via it. But concentrating at the lousy matters could make it revel in like you're reliving the experience. In addition to persevering with to get harm, it receives more hard to conquer the rejection.

Accept your feelings, however strive no longer to allow them to consume you. Keep it out of your steady communication and concept. Why? Our behaviors and expectations are delivered on with the beneficial aid of terrible thinking. Rejection can also want to even growth in case you live entrenched in a terrible frame of thoughts. It without a doubt discourages a person from giving it every extraordinary shot.

Track Listing for Examining Your Thought

Let's pay interest your opinion now: Take below consideration your justifications for being rejected Do you positioned yourself down too much? It is generally regular to ask why did it show up. You should reserve your justifications to the information whilst you offer yourself a proof.

Justify your moves by means of way of the use of announcing that to procure have emerge as down for prom because of the fact the individual did no longer need to go with you. Don't tell yourself things like "I'm the form of loser" or "I were given rejected due to the fact I'm now not attractive." None of those are real. They are overanalyzing the occasion and imagining a reason. Shut off any derogatory thoughts that could start to enter your head.

Self-blame or self-deprecating thoughts can accentuate our flaws and reason us to accept as true with topics about ourselves which can be without a doubt undeniable untrue. This way of wondering stifles hopes and self-self guarantee, which are sincerely what we need to transport beyond feeling lousy and preference to attempt all over again.

If you begin placing your self down or blaming your self for the rejection, you may begin to assume you could commonly be rejected. Illusions like "I'll in no way get a date" or "No one will ever like me" enlarge a easy rejection to the aspect of catastrophe. Even whilst rejection is probably pretty painful and demoralizing, it is not the give up of the location.

Maintaining Perspective

"Yeah, I had been given rejected this time," inform your self. Maybe I'll get a "certain" whilst next I in reality have the opportunity," or "Oh well. This is what took place. It bothers me. It's no longer how I had expected matters to go. However, rejection takes region to absolutely everyone, so I can attempt another time.

Think on your strengths and terrific traits. Keep in thoughts the sports at the same time as you received approval, made the reduce, or received a "sure." Consider all people who likes and helps you.

Reward your self in your efforts. It's first rate that you took a risk. Remember that you can deal with the rejection. Even despite the fact which you were rejected right now, there can be a few other hazard later. Get metaphysical Things sometimes arise for reasons that we do not usually understand.

Make the Most of Rejection

Rejection gives people the time to think about what they could beautify. It's appropriate to don't forget in which you can enhance or whether your goals were too lofty. Maybe you need to art work to your sport, your teachers, your interview approach, or some element it takes to boom your opportunities of having sizeable the following time in case your skills weren't robust enough this time. Make satisfactory you're making the maximum of the risk to get better by using the use of the usage of the rejection.

Chapter 6: The Consequences Of Rejection

So, right right right here's the unsightly reality: Rejection in a relationship has its traditional caution signs and symptoms Some subjects that your associate won't ever do to you until they are trying to inform you they may be now not inquisitive about the connection with you. Despite the obviousness of those warning flags, the worry of being deserted can maintain you in a dating for an prolonged period at the same time as you need to be going on together together with your existence.

The Consequences of Rejection and How to Get over the Fear of Rejection

Relationship rejection can be quite detrimental to the person that obtained it. For starters, humans would likely start experiencing rejection tension, which makes them approach any new connection with the concern that they'll speedy be rejected over again. On the alternative hand, rejection may additionally have untold terrible implications on a person's vanity. The character who became rejected can also need to have conceitedness problems for a while if they do no longer clearly get better.

Has someone rejected you? So that you could preserve dwelling your lifestyles, right proper here's the way to get over your fear of rejection.

1.   Don't allow it get to you

One of the hardest matters you will concentrate in recent times is surely this. Nevertheless, it needs to be said. To begin overcoming rejection in a relationship, you have to first famend that you had not anything to do with it.

2.   Give your self sufficient time to simply accept your emotions and get better.

It takes area frequently that the number one element you could do while you develop ill of being rejected in a courting is to head away and begin over. Rebounds, in accordance to research, are greater dangerous than beneficial. Take all of the time you want to heal after completing the poisonous relationship. Return to your self. Get new pursuits. More pals to make. Before you enter a modern-day dating, rediscover who you are and take accurate care of yourself.

three. A professional may be vital.

To sincerely recover from the consequences of relationships like the ones, you may every so often need professional assist. Now, consulting a professional is one method for overcoming the anxiety of being rejected in a romantic relationship. Consider consulting a therapist, psychologist, or highbrow health expert.

How To Manage the Pain of Rejection

We all looking for and require the capacity to revel in reputation, love, and being involved. It is one of the essential mental requirements for residing that begin in early life and keep all of the way to adulthood. Due to this, experiencing emotional forget about approximately of any type or diploma similarly to the concern of doing so are harsh and risky. And why it hurts even if a person you care approximately ignores you.

If any of those intellectual situations are inflicting you intellectual pressure right now, you may want to don't forget enrolling in a love dependancy in depth class in which you can take a look at techniques for reducing, accepting, and overcoming rejection ache. The first step in improving your emotional well-being is to get knowledge approximately the specifics of emotional rejection and the manner, if left out, they're able to have a negative effect in your lifestyles.

Why Does Rejection Lead to Obsession?

On the only hand, even the dread of being rejected with the aid of a person you care approximately, romantically or in some one-of-a-kind manner, can cause us to increase clingy and compulsive behavioral behavior.

On the possibility facet, there may be a biological justification for why rejection may result in obsessive behavior. The identical regions of our thoughts that keep us stimulated are stimulated thru manner of romantic rejection.

Additionally, it affects the regions of our mind which is probably associated with addiction, rewards, and cravings. This is the physiologic explanation for why you frequently enjoy sentiments of obsessive attachment after someone rejects you romantically.

There are certainly one of a kind techniques to account for this compulsive mental fashion, despite the fact that. For instance, you could receive as true with it is your fault and be making amends on your errors. Maybe you still trust that person to be your best healthy. Regardless of the reasons, rejection regularly has compulsive effects.

What Is the Best Way to Handle Rejection in A Relationship?

There are healthful, effective strategies to deal with emotional rejection. Without the beneficial aid of skilled courting advocates, your efforts to conquer love addiction may additionally from time to time fail. This have to now not, however, discourage you from in search of to apply the following strategies:

Consider Everything

Give yourself the high-priced of allowing all emotions to skip via you, each appropriate and horrible. Allow yourself to come upon each one. Avoid walking away from them or seeking to push them away. Accept them, and take movement to begin your rehabilitation.

Recognize The Pain

Be cautious no longer to enter denial. Be practical and take delivery of the fact that you could harm and that matters will fast turn out to be painful. The starting of the recovery device happens inside the course of this phase of comprehension and reputation.

Stop Blaming Yourself

People who're experiencing rejection regularly start blaming themselves right away on the equal time as idealizing the alternative person. But understand that it wasn't all of your fault. It takes to make a tango, and to interrupt one.

Give Yourself Some Mercy

Don't just prevent at abstaining from self-blame. Take it a step further and be kind to your self. Be in the agency of people who will assist and show you care. Do this due to the reality you want to have buddies who will recognize you and pay attention to you with out passing judgment, now not because of the fact you need all people's approval or reputation.

Keep It from Defining You

The unsightly emotions which can be presently circling spherical inner of you do not sincerely define who you are. You are greater than the suffering you are going thru and the person that emerge as certainly grew to end up down. Remember which you are greater than the manner you currently revel in.

Understand It

Learn from your reports in addition in your faults, inclusive of the manner you have been treated, how your relationships evolved, and the manner they ended. You'll locate comfort inside the idealistic, rose-colored photo in case you spend a while making it extra practical.

Never Be Afraid to Ask for Help

Finally, do no longer be afraid to ask for assistance. There are qualified relationship advocates who've the experience and recognize-a way to assist individuals who are experiencing similar troubles to you. A great variety of issues, together with rejection, emotional attachment, love addiction and fixation, and masses of others., may be addressed thru the use of specialists. They can guide you via it all and help you notice complicated behavioral styles that you could regulate.

How Can You Distinguish Your Self-Worth from Romantic Rejection?

One of the maximum painful kinds of rejection is romantic rejection. It pierces right through the middle of who we are and the manner attractive we anticipate we're. No one is exempt, each. Rejection is a fear that over 70% of people have, specifically as regards to their age and look. This confirms what girls have advised us.

The ache of a love rejection can final longer when you have low vanity or have professional trauma. Thankfully, most people can conquer the terrible emotions via counting on supportive buddies or circle of relatives. However, those folks who already be afflicted by using low arrogance and hold repressed reminiscences of youngsters trauma might also additionally experience delays of months, if now not years.

So, how can also we lessen our very personal struggling? We do no longer get alongside side without a doubt all of us we meet, let's accept it; if we did, we might be exceptional pals with absolutely everyone we've got were given ever met. Dating gives us the hazard to discover extra about who we're and what we want, further to to make bigger our resilience through interactions with each the right human beings and the wrong ones. Therefore, on the equal time as a person rejects you, the universe is guiding you towards suitable partners who're deserving of you, a while, and your love similarly to saving you valuable time. Therefore, rejection is beneficial because it every teaches us a few thing and pushes us in the direction of our goals and pleasure.

No one is rejecting you; the relationship is

Rejection in no manner has a selected purpose. If our accomplice breaks up with us, it's much more likely due to a trouble with the connection than it is to do with us specifically, she explains. "Separating our enjoy of self from the mixed self we end up whilst we bond with specific humans may be certainly empowering."

We additionally need to understand that rejection is in no manner truely non-public; it is often reflective of key wishes or goals that are not being met inside a mutual dynamic. Therefore, whilst a person breaks up with you or declines to pursue the connection further, it is no longer usually you as a person who is being rejected.

Chapter 7: Advantages Of Rejection

The regrettable however crucial trouble of the human enjoys is rejection. Whether or no longer they may be aware about it, absolutely everyone encounters rejection in some unspecified time in the future of their lives. The blessings of rejection are some component that many people who undergo this in no way surely recognize. This may also moreover appear counterintuitive, however sincerely ask anyone who has ever been became down for a process or had a loved one claim they had been now not interested in them that way. If you high-quality have a look at rejection the proper way, it could definitely be a quite useful problem most of the time. Here are 10 benefits of rejection you need to maintain in mind the following time you find out yourself on this situation.

1.   Being rejected inspires us to art work more difficult.

Rejection can be an illustration that you need to start doing something you are now not currently doing or stop performing some element you're now doing. You is probably on the street to doing higher and encountering an lousy lot much less rejection within the future while you discover what it's far.

2.   Rejection teaches us that we are simplest human.

Each individual is the celeb of their very very own story, that can purpose an comprehensible but fake experience of self-significance in the grand scheme of things. Everyone may additionally moreover want to want being knocked down a peg or in a few unspecified time in the destiny, consequently rejection is definitely an exquisite difficulty. No count how incredible we'd want to assume we are, rejection serves to remind us that we are all surely human.

three. Rejection lets in you increase endurance.

Rejection can are available many particular bureaucracy, some of that are painful at the identical time as others are downright catastrophic. One of the toughest rejections may be not getting the approach you spent a month sending resumes, emails, and faxes backward and forward for due to the reality the payments and the cabinet do not supply a rattling about your damaged feelings. Rejection, but, might in all likelihood teach you to be affected person and preserve moving into this case, so take advantage of it. Even notwithstanding the reality that you could not right away get maintain of what you want, in case you're prepared to put in the critical try to have staying power, you may finally arrive at your preferred vacation spot.

4.   Rejection evokes us to take alternative routes.

Rejection can sometimes be existence's manner of letting us comprehend that the excellent way to attain our goals is by way of method of selecting a tremendous path. The direction we are seeking to have a look at may not be the incredible one for us, or in all likelihood there can be a superior one which we haven't however determined. If you are willing to attempt a one in every of a type direction or find a new method to perform the identical reason, rejection can be a high-quality enjoy.

five.   Rejection makes us re-observe who we are.

Many people have problem accepting rejection. That is normal. Rejection hurts and is unpleasant. However, at the same time as a few element is repeated enough instances, humans normally start to pay interest. An example of one of these rejection is, "You're not too heat at managing different people, however you have were given extremely good abilities with numbers." One key advantage of rejection that human beings regularly overlook approximately is the capability to reinvent oneself through turning into extra intention- or human beings-orientated or with the aid of the usage of converting factors of our personalities to get alongside better with the ones spherical us.

6.   Rejection reasons us to reevaluate our targets.

The person who struggles via an MBA degree because of the truth they've got been informed their complete lives that it is the key to fulfillment and power even as what they actually need to do is play the violin in an orchestra is an instance of the manner as species, we often neglect warning signs and signs and symptoms which can be there for our benefit. After the interview, the candidate is knowledgeable that they have been egregiously underqualified. A 0.33-chair violinist is likewise wanted via the network orchestra. Your dreams will continually come thru, and sometimes rejection forces us to select most of the "secure motive" that could in the long run depart us unhappy and the impossibly difficult ambition we've got typically desired to pursue.

7.	Rejection offers probabilities for development.

Consider the final time someone claimed he should in no way have placed a device, met the character or moved to a place if the opportunity vicinity hadn't refused to rent him or someone hadn't refused to marry him or a town had extra jobs to be had. Rejection may be a robust motivator for us to take a look at why we pursue the dreams we do and what it is approximately them that motivates us to hold closer to, or abandon, the ones dreams. It also can be an superb possibility to mirror on why one pursues unique dreams, humans, positions, or times. As a race, we is probably hundreds happier and additional regular in our competencies and instincts if we would clearly take the time to pay attention to what these things are telling us approximately ourselves.

eight. Rejection opens our eyes to sparkling views.

Everybody every so often has tunnel vision. We provide all of our interest to a unmarried purpose, to someone, or to a dream. Rejection can strain one to take a step once more and reconsider one's desires and strategies for attaining them. In this case, it's miles vital to undertake a smooth attitude and do not forget possibility strategies to accomplishing the identical give up stop result similarly to how we view our personal aspirations and ambitions.

9.   Rejection makes us extra resilient.

There's an adage that the fish that swims upstream is the maximum powerful. Although rejection frequently appears to forestall you on your tracks, in reality it offers you some thing to push in opposition to. People do not end up more potent on the identical time as the whole lot is going their manner, but as an alternative when they should address the surprising or ugly. In this regard, rejection is useful since it demonstrates our real strength, resiliency, and potential underneath stress.

10.   Rejection presents a risk for improvement.

Rejection does now not continuously need to be a awful thing. Instead, keep in mind viewing rejection as an possibility so that you can growth in my opinion. Perhaps you find out via rejection that your aftershave motives sinus headaches or that your temperament in a professional placing turns human beings away. Any place of your lifestyles can experience the instructions you examine via rejection, at the manner that will help you become a more potent, nicer, and additional "polished" character.

You can envisage that rejection can be terrible, but it is able to moreover emerge as a blessing in cover. What remains to be visible is how you may reply to rejection. Will you capture the danger it is providing you with or have the skylight hooked up in your living room? Your selection is yours.

Chapter 8: The Everyday Sting Of Emotional Cuts And Scrapes

Rejection is a standard human experience. It may additionally sting like a slap inside the face or depart us feeling like our hearts have been ripped out. It can are available in various office work, from a failed mission interview to a love cut up, from a friend's careless phrases to a social snub.

The Pain of Rejection:

Rejection hurts because it sparks our deep-seated yearning for belonging and approval. When we are rejected, we experience lonely and on my own. We can also query our certainly actually really worth and fear if we are right enough. These sensations may be profoundly distressing and may take a toll on our vanity and self assurance.

The Everyday Rejections:

While some rejections are massive, existence-changing reports, many others are tiny, normal occurrences. These "micro-rejections" may be just as devastating, regardless of the reality that they may not experience as excessive. For example, being unnoticed in a communicate, receiving a harsh comment on social media, or being surpassed over for a advertising and marketing and advertising can all purpose emotions of rejection.

The Cumulative Effect:

Over time, even tiny rejections can have a cumulative impact. They can put on down our resistance and make us touchier to feeling disappointed and discouraged. This is why it's far crucial to apprehend how to address rejection successfully.

The Different Types of Rejection:

Rejection can are available many tactics, from the overt and obtrusive to the diffused and unspoken. Here are a handful of the maximum preferred varieties of rejection:

Social rejection: This can comprise being rejected from a set, being unnoticed in a verbal exchange, or being not noted of social sports.

Romantic rejection: This can include being rejected with the aid of manner of someone you're interested in, going via a breakup, or experiencing adultery.

Academic rejection: This can involve being rejected from a university or software program, acquiring a lousy mark, or being chastised in your art work.

Professional rejection: This can consist of getting surpassed over for a advertising, being laid off from your manner, or being rejected from a mission interview.

Family rejection: This can incorporate feeling along with you do not belong to your own family, being criticized with the useful resource of your own family people, or being separated from your own family.

The Impact of Rejection on Mental and Emotional Well-being:

Rejection may also have a outstanding have an impact on on our mental and emotional well-being. It can cause feelings of:

Sadness: Rejection can provoke emotions of sadness and loss, as we lament the loss of a dating, opportunity, or sense of belonging.

Anger: When we sense rejected, we may additionally moreover experience anger towards the person that rejected us or within the course of ourselves.

Shame: Rejection can reason feelings of disgrace and worthlessness, due to the truth we also can count on that we're come what also can imperfect or insufficient.

Anxiety: Rejection can create tension, as we worry approximately the future and the manner we are able to deal with the outcomes of rejection.

Depression: In a few conditions, rejection can turn out to be melancholy, that could be a essential highbrow fitness trouble that calls for expert help.

Reasons We May Be More Sensitive to Rejection:

There are masses of variables that may make us greater touchy to rejection. These include:

Our early research: If we have been rejected or chastised via way of our mother and father or caregivers, we may be greater susceptible to experience rejected in different factors of our lives.

Our arrogance: People with low shallowness are more inclined to take rejection in my opinion and to experience like it is a reflected picture of their sincerely properly well worth.

Our attachment fashion: People with worrying or avoidant attachment styles are much more likely to be touchy to rejection and to enjoy it greater profoundly.

Our persona: People who're introverted or exceedingly touchy may be greater willing to experience rejected in social situations.

Practical Techniques for Coping with Rejection:

Dealing with the emotional effect of rejection needs self-compassion and a healthful angle. Here are some useful strategies:

Allow your self to enjoy your feelings. Bottle the usage of your sentiments will simplest reason them to fester. Acknowledge your ache, express it healthily, and allow your self to grieve the loss.

Talk to a person you keep in mind. Sharing your enjoy with a being concerned buddy, family member, or therapist can provide emotional validation and beneficial recommendations.

Practice self-care. Prioritize sports that enhance your physical and intellectual properly-being, which encompass workout, rest strategies, and spending time in nature.

Focus for your strengths. Remind yourself of your immoderate first-rate attributes and accomplishments to beautify your self perception and conceitedness.

Seek professional help if wished. If you discover it tough to deal with rejection, try obtaining expert help from a therapist or counselor.

Rejection can be a wonderful fuel for non-public growth and transformation. By spotting its nature, dealing with its ache, and studying from it, you can emerge stronger and extra resilient than ever in advance than.

Remember that rejection does now not represent your sincerely truely really worth. It's handiest a diversion to your quest to self-discovery and success. Embrace the boundaries, analyze from the setbacks, and maintain to transport ahead with grace and perseverance.

A Story of Overcoming Rejection: Sarah's Journey from Job Loss to Reinvention

Sarah had continuously been a devoted and hardworking employee. For 15 years, she had poured her coronary coronary heart into her profession at a large enterprise business enterprise. She have turn out to be a valued part of the organization and felt confident in her function and future with the employer.

Then, in the destiny, everything changed. Sarah changed into known as into her supervisor's place of business and knowledgeable that her role became being abolished due to restructuring. She grow to be devastated. The statistics felt like successful inside the intestine, and she or he without delay started out out to impeach her definitely properly well worth and her capacity.

The Initial Shock:

The first severa weeks after her activity loss have been especially difficult. Sarah felt misplaced and directionless. She have turn out to be triumph over with emotions like rage, grief, and fear. She did now not apprehend in which to show or what to do subsequent.

The Sting of Rejection:

As Sarah started searching out new jobs, she met every unique wave of rejection. She modified into surpassed over for a couple of roles and felt like a failure. The rejections virtually helped to strengthen her awful feelings approximately herself.

Turning Point:

One day, at the same time as exploring the net, Sarah stumbled upon a internet site approximately company. She had commonly been interested by beginning her private organisation, however in no manner felt bold sufficient to make the leap. This turned into a turning point for Sarah. She understood that her method loss can be an possibility to in the long run pursue her ambition.

Embracing Change:

Sarah selected to make investments her severance settlement in launching her enterprise. She enrolled in online schooling, networked with other marketers, and produced a advertising and marketing method. It modified into some of tough art work, however Sarah come to be decided to reap achievement.

Building Resilience:

Sarah skilled severa hurdles alongside the street. There were days while she doubted herself and favored to surrender. But she remembered the brink of rejection and the manner it had inspired her to alternate her existence. She drew strength from her reports and applied them to energy her willpower.

The Power of Reinvention:

After a 12 months of hard work and resolution, Sarah's industrial enterprise employer turned into a success. She changed into in the long run her boss and performing some element she favored. The stumble upon had no longer best impacted her project however furthermore her life. She had emerge as a more resilient and confident individual.

Lessons Learned:

Sarah's story is an superb example of techniques rejection can be a catalyst for boom and exchange. It shows us that even the maximum tough sports can be opportunities to research and develop.

Here are a few important classes from Sarah's story:

Rejection is a ordinary element of life.

Rejection does now not outline us.

We may study from rejection and boom stronger.

Rejection may be an possibility to comply with our aspirations.

If you're suffering with the brink of rejection, bear in mind Sarah's tale. Be slight to yourself, have a look at from your opinions, and do no longer be scared to rebuild your existence.

Chapter 9: When Our Relationship Muscles Grow Weak

Loneliness is a popular human sensation. It's the sensation of solitude and alienation from others. It's a longing for massive connections and a revel in of belonging.

While once in a while loneliness is suitable, chronic loneliness may additionally have a intense effect on our physical and intellectual health. It can boom the threat of sadness, anxiety, and in all likelihood coronary coronary heart disorder.

What Causes Loneliness?

Several reasons can contribute to loneliness. Some of the maximum commonplace encompass:

Social isolation: This may be attributed to events inclusive of living by myself, running from home, or having inclined social abilties.

Loss of cherished ones: The lack of life of a partner, family member, or close to buddy can reason acute loneliness.

Relationship troubles: Conflict, betrayal, or a loss of intimacy in our relationships can make contributions to emotions of loneliness.

Mental fitness troubles: Depression, anxiety, and different intellectual health situations could make it difficult to interact with others and may reason social isolation.

Life transitions: Moving to a brand new region, starting a brand new manner, or having children may additionally furthermore all be lonely reviews.

Signs of Loneliness:

Loneliness can show in severa tactics, however a few not unusual signs and symptoms embody:

Feeling secluded and on my own, even supposing surrounded with the useful resource of the usage of people.

Yearning for actual connections and partnerships.

Feeling consisting of you don't belong.

Withdrawing from social sports sports.

Engaging in awful self-communicate.

Feeling forlorn or despairing.

Building Resilience Against Loneliness:

There are numerous topics you can do to assemble resilience in opposition to loneliness. Here are some pointers:

Nurture present day relationships: Make time for the individuals who depend maximum to you. Make an investment to your ties on your circle of relatives and friends.

Expand your social circle: Join golf equipment, organizations, or businesses that interest you. Take instructions or workshops to satisfy new people.

Volunteer some time: Helping others is a wonderful manner to connect to your community and meet new pals.

Practice self-care: Engage in self-care with the aid of searching after your bodily and emotional health. This will assist you feel higher and more assured, which could make it much much less hard to connect to others.

Be quality to your self: Loneliness is a not unusual human revel in. Don't blame yourself for feeling lonely.

Seek professional assist: If you're suffering to address loneliness, do not hesitate to seek professional guide. A therapist can provide you with help and help.

Remember, you aren't by myself. Loneliness is a not unusual suffering, and there are numerous equipment available that will help you deal.

A Story of Building Connection: David's Path from Isolation to Community

David has always been a loner. He preferred the enterprise of books to that of people and determined social interactions draining and hard. As a end end result, he spent maximum of his time alone, feeling on my own and unconnected with the world round him.

This solitude started out out to take a toll on David's mental and emotional nicely-being. He felt dejected, involved, and hopeless. He started out to trust that there was some thing incorrect with him and that he may usually be by myself.

One day, David stumbled upon a brochure for a nearby beneficial aid corporation for humans with social tension. He nervously selected to attend a meeting, unsure of what to expect.

At the assembly, David decided a set of individuals who understood his challenges. They were nice, accepting, and non-judgmental. They shared their personal stories of isolation and loneliness and presented assist and encouragement to every one-of-a-kind.

David felt like he belonged for the primary time ever. He decided that he wasn't on my own and that wonderful people understood how he felt.

As David endured to wait the aid group, he commenced to reinforce his social competencies. He placed the way to begin discussions, create small chats, and construct relationships. He additionally commenced to combat his horrible self-beliefs and installation a greater high-quality self-photograph.

Over time, David's social anxiety started out to disappear. He were given extra comfortable interacting with others and began to boom friendships outdoor of the useful resource institution. He joined a analyzing membership, started out volunteering at a neighborhood animal refuge, or perhaps started relationship.

Today, David is a selected man or woman. He continues to be introverted, however he enjoys spending time with others and has created a stable social useful resource community. He is no longer lonely and remoted, and he's appreciative of the guide organisation that assisted him on his road to connection and network.

Lessons Learned:

David's tale is an inspirational example of techniques it is feasible to overcome loneliness and boom great connections with others. It teaches us that:

We aren't by myself in our worrying conditions. Many human beings endure loneliness and social anxiety.

There is desire. With the first-class assist, we're capable of have a take a look at to conquer those problems and collect a profitable lifestyles.

Connection is vital for our nicely-being. We want wholesome relationships to thrive physically and emotionally.

It takes effort and time. Building resilience and overcoming loneliness is a adventure, no longer a destination.

There is manual available. Support businesses, remedy, and distinctive services can beneficial resource us in our quest for connection.

If you are preventing with loneliness, keep in mind David's tale. There is wish for you too.

Loss and Trauma: Walking on Broken Bones

Life is whole of americaand downs, pleasure and sorrow. But some encounters leave us with deeper wounds than others. Loss and trauma are two such situations that may have a fantastic effect on our lives.

Loss is the enjoy of being robbed of some thing big to us. This can contain the loss of a loved one, a career, a relationship, or really a sense of protection. Loss may be unexpected and surprising, or it may be a sluggish technique.

Trauma is a totally upsetting or disturbing revel in that overwhelms our ability to control. It is probably due to a unmarried incident, along with a automobile twist of destiny or natural disaster, or it can be the end result of sustained exposure to worrying or dangerous sports, like as abuse or forget about approximately.

The Impact of Loss and Trauma

Loss and trauma may additionally have a tremendous effect on our bodily and intellectual health. They can bring about numerous symptoms, together with:

Post-worrying strain sickness (PTSD): This is a intellectual fitness contamination that would growth following exposure to a stressful event. Symptoms of PTSD embody flashbacks, nightmares, anxiety, and depression.

Grief: This is a herbal reaction to loss. Symptoms of grief embody sadness, anger, guilt, and loneliness.

Depression: This is a highbrow health infection characterized through the use of emotions of melancholy, hopelessness, and lack of hobby in as quickly as interesting matters.

Anxiety: This is a sensation of hysteria, apprehension, or unease. Symptoms of anxiety encompass a pounding coronary coronary coronary heart, perspiration, and hassle slumbering.

Physical fitness issues: Loss and trauma can also contribute to physical health issues, together with coronary heart sickness, excessive blood strain, and chronic ache.

Coping with Loss and Trauma

Coping with loss and trauma is a difficult but important manner. There is not any right or incorrect way to grieve, and absolutely everyone heals at their tempo. However, high quality healthful coping strategies can assist us address ugly activities. These encompass:

Therapy can offer you with a constant and supportive location to method your feelings and increase healthy coping mechanisms.

Joining a manual group: Support companies can create a experience of network and reference to others who've lengthy beyond thru comparable conditions.

Practicing self-care: Self-care is crucial for each our physical and emotional well-being. Make sure you have got turn out to be adequate sleep, consuming wholesome food, and workout frequently.

Engaging in sports sports you revel in: Make time for hobbies that supply you delight and rest.

Connecting with loved ones: Spending time with cherished ones can bring useful resource and comfort

Practicing mindfulness: Mindfulness can allow us to interest on the present second and receive our thoughts and feelings with out judgment.

Understanding which you aren't by myself is essential. Loss and trauma are normal reviews, and there are various machine to be had that will help you deal. Do now not hesitate to invite for help if you want it.

A Story of Healing: Maria's Transformation after a Traumatic Experience

Maria's existence changed into vivacious and entire of choice. A talented younger artist with a loving family and supportive pals, she emanated joy and optimism. But her international collapsed the day she witnessed a horrible incident. The incident left her feeling shattered and damaged plagued with fear, worry, and guilt.

The days that accompanied have been a whirl of nightmares, flashbacks, and overwhelming feelings. Maria withdrew from the area, distancing herself from her cherished ones and abandoning her passions. She felt misplaced and on my own, handling the load of the trauma and the guilt she held for not being able to assist.

However, internal Maria's coronary coronary heart, a spark of resistance flickered. Despite the darkness, she refused to surrender to melancholy. She understood she had to find out a manner to get higher and rebuild her life.

Seeking Support:

Maria began her route via way of looking for expert remedy. A therapist supplied her with a constant area to gadget her emotions and increase suitable coping techniques. Through treatment, she located out to manipulate her anxiety, address her guilt, and get better manipulate over her existence.

Reconnecting with Creativity:

Maria additionally reconnected together collectively with her love for paintings. Painting have come to be her catharsis, a manner to speak the agony and trauma she carried inner. As she spilled her feelings onto the canvas, she started out to peer the sector through sparkling eyes, locating beauty and optimism amidst the darkness.

Embracing Forgiveness:

Perhaps the most tough step for Maria modified into gaining knowledge of to forgive herself. She blamed herself for now not being capable of keep away from the awful occasion, carrying a wonderful enjoy of guilt. Through therapy and self-compassion, she often determined out to forgive herself and allow move of the shame that had held her once more.

Finding Strength in Community:

Maria additionally decided braveness and concept in interacting with others who had confronted trauma. Sharing her story and paying attention to their stories helped her understand she wasn't on my own. She determined peace inside the shared enjoy and the information of individuals who had walked a comparable direction.

A New Chapter:

Today, Maria is a unique man or woman. The scars of trauma continue to be, however they now not define her. She has converted her ache proper right into a first rate strain for restoration and growth. Maria maintains to make artwork, the use of her platform to elevate popularity about trauma and inspire folks that are suffering.

Lessons Learned:

Maria's tale is a monument to the human spirit's strength for recuperation and transformation. It teaches us that:

Trauma may be a stimulus for development. While painful, traumatic recollections also can purpose top notch human growth and self-discovery.

Healing is viable. No count quantity how deep the injuries, recovery is manageable with time, attempt, and the precise assist.

Seeking beneficial resource is a sign of power. Asking for expert assistance is a key step in the restoration approach.

Creativity may be a superb tool for recovery. Expressing emotions via art work, tune, or one-of-a-kind cutting-edge avenues may be a therapeutic and provoking experience.

Forgiveness is important for going in advance. Letting rid of guilt and resentment permits us to heal and flow into on with our lives.

Community and connection are crucial. Sharing our tale and connecting with others who have had comparable problems can offer critical help and encouragement.

Maria's story offers need to certainly all of us who has faced trauma. It reminds us that we are not by me and that restoration and transformation are feasible.

Chapter 10: The Poison We Carry Within

Guilt is a powerful feeling that might have a superb impact on our lives. It is a experience of guilt or remorse for a few factor we have accomplished or didn't perform. Unlike disgrace, which makes a speciality of our feel of self esteem, guilt focuses on our deeds.

While guilt can serve a characteristic through the usage of using us to make amends and adjust our behavior, it can moreover become a terrible force, fundamental to emotions of disgrace, isolation, and depression.

The Origins of Guilt:

Guilt may be produced via the usage of a multitude of circumstances, which includes:

Moral transgressions: When we breach our ethical code or do a little detail that we agree with is inaccurate, we may additionally go through guilt.

Social expectations: We can also experience responsible whilst we fail to meet the expectations of others, even though such expectations are unjustified.

Childhood critiques: Our early reviews with punishment and praise would possibly impact our idea of proper and incorrect and make contributions to emotions of shame.

Trauma: Traumatic conditions can motive feelings of guilt, specially if we revel in accountable for what befell.

The Impact of Guilt:

Guilt may additionally have a massive have an impact on on on our physical and emotional health. It can purpose:

Depression: Persistent emotions of guilt may also make a contribution to the improvement of despair.

Anxiety: Guilt can cause us to worry and ruminate on the beyond, resulting in tension.

Isolation: When we're fed on with the aid of using guilt, we can also retreat from social connection and distance ourselves from others.

Low vanity: Guilt can motive bad self-ideals and feelings of worthlessness.

Physical fitness worries: Chronic stress and fear produced by way of guilt can bring about physical health problems, which includes complications, stomachaches, and exhaustion.

Finding Freedom from Guilt:

Fortunately, there are strategies to benefit comfort from guilt and pass on with our lives. Here are a few steps you can take:

1. Acknowledge your guilt. The first step to mending is to renowned your guilt. Don't attempt to suppress or overlook approximately your sentiments.

2. Take responsibility. If you are answerable for a few aspect you possibly did, take obligation on your moves. This does not suggest you need to beat yourself up,

however it does recommend acknowledging your characteristic in the hassle.

three. Make amends. If possible, try and atone for your acts. This may also need to include apologizing to someone you injured, correcting a mistake, or making efforts to prevent something similar from happening once more.

4. Forgive yourself. This is often the toughest degree, but it's far critical for recovery. Forgive your self on your errors and understand that everyone makes them.

five. Seek help. Talking to a therapist or counselor can provide massive help and direction as you flow thru your guilt.

6. Practice self-compassion. Treat your self with care and understanding. Remember which you are human, and you're sincerely worth of forgiveness.

7. Focus on the present. Don't linger at the beyond. Instead, consciousness at the

prevailing moment and create a brighter future for yourself.

Remember, you are not on my own. We all face guilt once in a while. By spotting its motives and gaining knowledge of a way to manipulate it, we can benefit liberation from its grip and create a more worthwhile lifestyles.

A Story of Forgiveness: John's Path to Letting Go of Guilt and Shame

John had a wonderful load — a weight of remorse and humiliation that had plagued him for years. The recollections of his previous sins tormented him, preventing him from shifting forward and finding happiness.

His existence starts offevolved with a succession of terrible choices, errors advocated with the aid of way of rage and contempt. These choices led him down a route of self-destruction, causing struggling and struggling now not just to himself but moreover to those he loved. As the ramifications of his actions discovered out, John became plagued via guilt and disgrace.

He withdrew from his cherished ones, burying himself in a worldwide of regret. He attempted to drown his grief with drink and one of a kind distractions, however the guilt simplest worsened. John felt trapped, no longer capable of forgive himself or find out any shape of serenity.

One day, however, a ray of optimism surfaced. John stumbled and located a e-book about forgiveness. As he look at the chapters, he received a clean attitude. He started out out to understand that forgiveness wasn't approximately approving his behavior, but about releasing himself from the emotional prison he had made for himself.

The path in the path of forgiveness come to be extended and tough. John needed to confront his demons, admit the harm he had triggered, and take duty for his options. He sought guidance from a therapist, who helped him paintings thru his feelings and build particular coping mechanisms.

Slowly, with every stride he made, John felt lighter. The burden of guilt started to lessen, replaced with the resource of a renewed experience of self-compassion and statistics. He located out to forgive himself no longer through removing the beyond, but with the beneficial aid of accepting it as a part of his tale.

As John got here to forgive himself, he changed into additionally capable of forgive those who had wronged him. He diagnosed that defensive onto hatred and resentment handiest injured him in the long run. Letting go allowed him to move ahead with a lighter coronary heart and create extra healthy relationships.

John's adventure of forgiveness changed into transformative. He emerged from the darkness a wonderful guy, loose from the shackles of guilt and humiliation. He decided peace inner himself and reconnected with the people he cherished. He determined out to consist of his shortcomings and phrase himself as worthy of love and happiness.

John's tale is an uplifting monument to the strength of forgiveness. It teaches us that:

We all make mistakes. No one is first rate, and all and sundry has made alternatives they regret in a few unspecified time in the future.

Forgiveness is viable. Even the maximum deeply ingrained guilt and shame can be removed thru forgiveness.

Forgiveness is a preference. It calls for try and backbone, but it's miles a desire we will all make.

Forgiveness liberates us. By forgiving ourselves and others, we relieve ourselves from the emotional burdens that hold us back.

Forgiveness allows us to heal and flourish. When we forgive, we open ourselves to new opportunities and a brighter future.

If you're scuffling with with guilt or shame, take into account John's tale. There is desire for recovery and forgiveness. You aren't on my own, and also you need to find peace.

Rumination: Picking on the Scabs of Emotional Pain

Rumination is the act of specializing in horrible thoughts, emotions, and occasions. It's like scratching at a scab that might not heal, keeping us from transferring beforehand and taking element in pride.

When we ruminate, we get locked in a loop of negativity. We replay beyond sports in our brains, that specialize in our faults, regrets, and screw ups. We dissect every phrase and motion, emphasizing our flaws and picturing all the techniques topics may additionally moreover have prolonged long beyond in any other case.

This persistent repetition of negativity may have a profound have an effect on on on our intellectual and emotional nicely-being. It can motive:

Increased tension and depression: Rumination is a number one threat issue for tension and melancholy. The more we linger on bad thoughts, the much more likely we're to collect tremendous mental health issues.

Low shallowness: When we time and again live on our defects and mistakes, it erodes our conceitedness and makes us enjoy worthless.

Decision fatigue: Rumination can tire our intellectual belongings, making it hard to make alternatives and attention on the prevailing time.

Missed opportunities: When we're consumed via our horrible mind, we skip over out on possibilities for happiness and connection.

Breaking the Cycle of Rumination:

Fortunately, there are approaches to disrupt the cycle of ruminating and release ourselves from its grip. Here are a few useful strategies:

Identify your triggers: What are the situations or mind that lead you to ruminate? Once you recognize your triggers, you could build strategies to avoid them or healthily manage them.

Examine your negative thoughts: When you find out yourself lingering on horrible thoughts, study their veracity. Are those mind sensible? Are they beneficial? Are there alternate strategies of searching on the state of affairs?

Practice mindfulness: Mindfulness is the sector of specializing inside the triumphing second without judgment. Mindfulness sports activities can let you detach from your thoughts and feelings and become more privy to your inner enjoy with out becoming stuck up in it.

Engage in sports activities you revel in: Doing sports activities you experience can help in retaining your thoughts off of your poor thoughts and lift your temper.

Connect with others: Talking to a truthful friend, member of the family, or therapist can offer assist and could will let you get mindset for your state of affairs.

Practice self-compassion: Remember that everyone makes errors. Be kind and statistics to yourself, and do now not be afraid to invite for assist whilst you want it.

It is vital to undergo in thoughts that breaking the cycle of rumination requires time and effort. Don't emerge as discouraged if you experience setbacks. Keep the usage of those techniques, and in the end, you'll find out that you could allow pass of awful thoughts and pass in advance at the aspect of your lifestyles.

A Story of Mindfulness: Lisa's Journey from Rumination to Acceptance

Lisa modified into a prisoner in her mind. Trapped in a loop of consistent rumination, she replayed beyond mistakes and concerns, compounding them into insurmountable duties. Every misstep, each perceived failure, fuelled the flames of her pessimism, burning away her joy and peace.

She needed to get away the tyranny of her thoughts and find out a course to internal peace. But the continual chattering of her thoughts made it almost not viable to interest at the cutting-edge second or enjoy the tremendous subjects in her lifestyles.

One day, a pal added Lisa to the exercising of mindfulness. At first, she modified into doubtful. Could without a doubt focusing on her breath and physiological sensations definitely quell the typhoon interior her?

With an open mind, Lisa started out attending mindfulness meditation commands. Slowly, she commenced out to feel a shift. As she focused on her breath, she located the thoughts flowing in her mind without judgment. She found to widely known them with out becoming over excited of their emotional flow.

With practice, Lisa determined a newfound distance among her mind and her reactions. She discovered out to recognize her thoughts and feelings as short sports, now not everlasting realities. She determined to allow skip of the past and acquire the contemporary-day second.

The transition emerge as slow however dramatic. The incessant rumination that had plagued her for years began out to decrease. She started to apprehend the simple joys of life, the warm temperature of the solar on her pores and pores and pores and skin, the laughter of a toddler, and the splendor of a sunset.

Lisa's journey to mindfulness wasn't with out its hurdles. There had been days whilst the lousy ideas resurfaced, searching for to take her lower back into the darkness. But with each setback, she discovered to be greater affected person and compassionate with herself.

She ordinary the location of self-compassion, treating oneself with care and records She understood that everybody makes mistakes and that her terrible perspectives failed to decide her actually properly well worth.

As Lisa went on her route, she began to reconstruct her existence. She reunited with misplaced pals, pursued her passions, and opened her coronary heart to new possibilities. She observed to truely accept herself, flaws and all, and finished a revel in of serenity and contentment she had by no means felt earlier than.

Lisa's story is a testomony to the transformative power of mindfulness and self-compassion. It teaches us that:

We aren't our mind. Our mind are only ephemeral events, not eternal realities.

We can learn how to have a look at our thoughts without judgment. This lets in us to disconnect from the negativity and find out serenity.

Self-compassion is essential for restoration. When we address ourselves with kindness and empathy, we may additionally moreover begin to permit skip of preceding errors and circulate ahead with our lives.

The present day 2nd is all we have. By that specialize in the gift second; we're able to find out pride and peace, regardless of what occurred in the beyond or what also can show up inside the destiny.

Mindfulness is a adventure, no longer a holiday spot. There might be u.S.And downs, but with normal try, we can discover a way to silence the inner critic and nurture internal calm.

If you're suffering with with rumination or terrible mind, consider Lisa's story. There is choice for restoration and peace. By studying to be thoughtful and compassionate with yourself, you may stop the cycle of negativity and create a better and greater nice life.

Chapter 11: Turning Setbacks Into Stepping Stones

Failure is a part of life. It's inescapable, unavoidable, and often unwanted. But what if we modified our mind-set on failure? What if, as opposed to perceiving it as a setback, we seemed it as a threat for increase and getting to know?

The Power of Reframing Failure:

Our notion of failure determines our attitude to it. When we regard failure as a terrible and defining event, it may bring about discouragement, self-doubt, and a fear of taking risks. However, whilst we reframe failure as a getting to know opportunity, it is able to come to be a fantastic motivator for boom and self-development.

How Failure Can Help Us Grow:

Failure can educate us beneficial commands in severa techniques:

1. It highlights our shortcomings. Failure suggests places in which we want to enhance.

By identifying the ones deficiencies, we're able to bring together unique techniques to conquer them and end up greater in a function.

2. It builds resilience. Overcoming setbacks fosters resilience, the capability to get better from adversity. Each time we are dealing with and overcome a hassle, we get stronger and additional decided.

three. It fosters inventiveness. Failure can pressure us to expect outside the box and come up with new ideas. When our preliminary technique does no longer artwork, we're pushed to research one of a kind strategies, regularly essential to precise and innovative discoveries.

four. It develops self-interest. Failure can be a humbling revel in, pushing us to confront our boundaries and preconceptions. This self-cognizance can bring about better private growth and improvement.

5. It builds character. Overcoming adversities fosters perseverance, grit, and determination. These capabilities are essential for obtaining achievement in any trouble of existence.

Turning Failure into Stepping Stones:

Here are some techniques to convert failure into stepping stones:

1. Embrace the setback. Acknowledge and take shipping of the failure with out obsessing about it. Don't try to overlook about it or blame yourself.

2. Analyze what went wrong. Take the time to investigate the reasons of your failure. What have been the elements that contributed to it? What must you have got carried out in a exceptional way?

3. Learn out of your mistakes. Once you apprehend what went wrong, use that know-how to higher your future typical overall performance. Don't repeat the same mistakes.

4. Develop a growth mind-set. Believe that you can have a look at and develop out of your errors. Embrace obstacles and setbacks as possibilities to develop your competencies and information.

five. Seek feedback and useful resource. Talk to mentors, buddies, or colleagues for remarks and help. Their observations would possibly in all likelihood help you understand your deficiencies and increase techniques for boom.

6. Celebrate minor successes. Don't stay up for massive triumphs to have a terrific time. Recognize and applaud your development, no matter how tiny. This will hold you recommended and inspired to maintain moving forward.

Recall that experiencing failure is a ordinary a part of studying. By embracing it and reading from our mistakes, we are able to flip setbacks into stepping stones at the way to fulfillment.

A Story of Perseverance: Tom's Path to Success Through Failure

Tom modified into in no way taken into consideration the "brightest" or the "most gifted." He had trouble at faculty with subjects that others placed easy, and he often felt insufficient and discouraged. He fantasized about being a a success entrepreneur, however his contemporaries or even a few family participants appeared his dreams as unachievable.

Despite the uncertainties and criticism surrounding him, Tom refused to give up on his aspirations. He believed in himself and his abilties, although others did no longer He regular failure as a mastering possibility, now not a setback.

Tom's entrepreneurial journey have come to be some distance from clean He skilled several failures and rejections. He set up groups that failed, out of region coins, and confronted innumerable failures. Yet, through all of it, he endured. He placed from each failure, adjusted his techniques, and never left out his pursuits.

Tom's Secret Ingredients:

Several primary variables contributed to Tom's achievement:

1. Unwavering notion in himself: Despite the vitriol he professional, Tom in no way doubted his competencies. He had a deep-seated perception in himself and his capability to gain his desires.

2. Unrelenting perseverance: Tom in no way gave up, even if matters had been given hard. He addressed each problem head-on, refusing to permit setbacks dissuade him from his path.

3. A boom mind-set: Tom taken into consideration failure as a reading opportunity, not a defeat. He exploited each setback to discover his deficiencies and broaden his abilties.

4. A willingness to have a look at: Tom have become constantly equipped to research and improvement. He examine books, attended workshops, and sought out mentors who may manual him on his quest.

5. An constructive thoughts-set: Despite the hurdles he confronted, Tom maintained a happy mind-set. He centered at the opportunities and believed that he may need to achieve something he set his mind to.

Tom's Transformation:

Over time, Tom's hard paintings and determination paid off. He found out from his failures, subtle his capabilities, and sooner or later placed achievement. His business sports blossomed, and he attained economic freedom and personal achievement.

Tom's tale is a monument to the energy of tenacity and belief in oneself. It tells us that even within the face of adversity, fulfillment is achievable for individuals who are prepared to art work tough and in no manner give up on their aspirations.

Lessons Learned:

Tom's tale teaches us numerous critical lessons:

Never underestimate your capability. Have faith to your very very own abilities and your ability to be successful.

Don't allow others outline your bounds. Ignore the horrible and attention on proving your naysayers wrong.

Embrace failure as a mastering possibility. Learn out of your mistakes and get stronger from them.

Never surrender for your goals: regardless of how tough topics get, preserve going in advance, and never lose sight of your objectives.

Chapter 12: Strengthening Our Emotional Immune System

Low self-esteem is a general problem that influences human beings of every age and backgrounds. It is a terrible judgment of oneself, often characterized thru feelings of inadequacy, worthlessness, and absence of self warranty.

The Impact of Low Self-Esteem:

Low vanity may have a large effect on our existence. It can cause:

Depression and anxiety: People with horrible vanity are more likely to enjoy depression and anxiety.

Social isolation: Low self-esteem should make it hard to assemble and maintain healthy connections.

Poor decision-making: Low shallowness can cause terrible desire-making, in particular in regions alongside facet relationships and expert alternatives.

Substance abuse: People with horrible vanity may additionally flip to pills or alcohol to address their unpleasant emotions.

Physical health issues: Low conceitedness has been related to severa bodily health troubles, which incorporates coronary coronary heart sickness, stroke, and diabetes.

Strengthening Your Emotional Immune System:

Fortunately, there are subjects you could do to boom your conceitedness and installation a more potent emotional immune gadget. Here are some beneficial techniques:

1. Identify your awful mind: Pay interest to the terrible thoughts you've got were given got approximately your self. Once you discover them, task their legitimacy. Are the ones mind realistic? Are they beneficial? Are there alternate methods of looking on the scenario?

2. Practice self-compassion: Treat oneself with kindness and empathy. Remember that

everyone makes errors and which you aren't any exception.

3. Enjoy your successes: Take time to observe and experience your victories, irrespective of how minor. This will help you set up a greater immoderate high-quality self-photograph.

4. Focus on your strengths: Everyone has strengths and shortcomings. Make a listing of your strengths and art work to beautify them.

5. Be in the organisation corporation of wonderful human beings: Spend time with individuals who provide you with self guarantee in yourself. Avoid folks that are vital or judgmental.

6. Set sensible goals: Set goals which might be difficult but possible. Achieving your goals will offer you a experience of achievement and growth your self-self belief.

7. Seek professional assist: If you're scuffling with with low arrogance, do not hesitate to are trying to find expert help. A therapist can

give you assist and course on the same time as you try and decorate yourself-picture.

Improving self-esteem takes time and art work. Be affected individual with your self and do now not become disheartened if you enjoy setbacks. Keep making use of those procedures and you may regularly see accurate adjustments on your arrogance and ordinary nicely-being.

A Story of Self-Love: Anna's Journey from Doubt to Confidence

Anna come to be a girl in continual doubt her mind, a perpetual echo chamber of self-grievance, at a loss for words her every flow into, her each choice. She craved confidence, but it remained elusive, a shimmering mirage at the horizon of her fantasies.

Haunted via manner of way of lack of confidence, Anna lived a life of self-deprecation. She shied a protracted manner from opportunities, fearing failure and criticism. Social gatherings crammed her with dread, the highlight of interest an uncomfortable burden. Her voice, often complete of self-doubt, was now not frequently heard, her promise veiled underneath layers of dread and timidity.

One day, but, Anna stumbled upon a ebook about self-love. As she grew to become the pages, a spark of desire kindled inside her. The idea of self-popularity, of loving her shortcomings and honoring her specific talents, resonated deeply within her soul.

Anna began out on a voyage of self-discovery. She commenced to question her terrible idea styles, changing them with affirmations of self esteem. She got here to recognise her body, no longer for its perceived imperfections, however for its power and tenacity.

She pursued sports activities sports that furnished her pride, fostering her abilties and interests. She surrounded herself with encouraging partners, who contemplated her nicely really worth and advocated her to move outdoor her comfort place.

Slowly, but slowly, Anna's self assure commenced out to make bigger. The voice of self-doubt, as quickly as a booming roar, reduced to a faint whisper. She started to talk up, her voice gaining readability and self assure. She embraced adversities, remodeling them into stepping stones on her journey to development.

The worry of judgment failed to evaporate really, however it no longer paralyzed her. Anna discovered to recognize useful grievance from terrible negativity and to make use of the preceding to decorate, not lessen herself.

As Anna embarked on her journey of self-love, she located a clean freedom. The chains of self-doubt that had chained her for good-bye were broken. She stood tall, her head held immoderate, embracing her real self with unflinching self perception.

Anna's story is a tribute to the transformative energy of self-love. It suggests us that:

Self-love is a tool, now not a vacation spots It goals ongoing work and workout.

Self-recognition is the inspiration of self assurance. When we get hold of ourselves, flaws, and all, we are capable of begin to set up actual self-esteem.

We are all worth of affection, along with ourselves. Self-love isn't always a narcissistic act, however a critical step to live a happy and full existence.

Surrounding ourselves with great human beings can be a strong cause for transformation.

Confidence is a muscle that may be reinforced with workout. By venturing outside our comfort zones and taking possibilities, we can also grow our self belief and advantage our desires.

Anna's tale reminds us that interior each one mother and father lies the capability for self-love and self notion. By embarking on our paths of self-discovery and reputation, we may unharness our ability and stay our lives to the fullest.

Chapter 13: The Key To Sustainable Resilience

Resilience is usually described because the functionality to get better from problem. However, bouncing once more is certainly one part of the puzzle. True resilience additionally includes self-compassion, the capability to deal with oneself with care and information, mainly at some point of difficult times.

Why Self-Compassion Matters:

Self-compassion performs a vital feature in growing sustained resilience for numerous reasons:

1.   It reduces tension and anxiety. When we exercise self-compassion, we spark off the "soothing device" in our brains, which permits to soothe our nerves and decrease strain and tension.

2.   It fosters self-reputation. Self-compassion permits us to surely take delivery of our shortcomings and imperfections, in location of criticizing ourselves harshly. This self-splendor is crucial for developing a robust feeling of self confidence.

3.   It drives us to strive all once more. When we warfare, self-compassion allows us to be more forgiving of ourselves and encourages us to keep trying, despite the fact that we go through setbacks.

4.   It improves emotional nicely-being. Self-compassion enables to defend us from developing negative emotions including despair, fear, and anger.

Building Your Self-Compassion Muscle:

Like any capability, self-compassion desires exercise. Here are a few measures you may take to develop it:

1.   Become aware about your awful self-speak. Be privy to the horrible thoughts you have got about your self. Once you turn out

to be aware of them, have a observe their veracity and replace them with more sympathetic thoughts.

2. Treat your self with kindness. Talk to yourself the manner you may communicate to a chum who's going through a lousy period. Offer terms of encouragement and help.

three. Practice mindfulness. Mindfulness meditation will can help you grow to be extra privy to your thoughts and emotions without judgment. This can allow you to disengage from terrible self-talk and assemble a more loving picture of your self.

four. Remember that everyone makes mistakes. It's vital to recollect that mistakes are a everyday element of being human. Don't beat your self up about them. Instead, analyze from them and waft on.

5. Practice self-care. Attend in your emotional and bodily necessities. This have to include getting notable sufficient sleep, eating

nutritious food, exercising regularly, and appealing in sports activities you revel in.

6.   Seek assist from others. Discuss your difficulties with a dependable member of the family, pal, or therapist. Talking to someone who is conscious can be a extraordinary deliver of useful resource and encouragement.

Building self-compassion is a ordinary journey. Be affected character with yourself and applaud your development along the way. With persistent practice, you may create a deep properly of self-compassion that will let you weather any typhoon and emerge more potent than in advance than.

A Story of Self-Acceptance: Michael's Path to Embracing Imperfection

Michael have become a perfectionist. His lifestyles become a painstaking tapestry crafted from ambition and a tireless pursuit of immaculate success. He driven for impeccability in all elements of his lifestyles, from his profession to his relationships, continuously looking to be the high-quality.

However, this ordinary quest for perfection came at a value. Michael lived in continual fear of failure, his self confidence related to his accomplishments. He not regularly relished the current-day second, continuously centered on the subsequent aim, the next triumph. He studied each disorder, each perceived imperfection, in himself and others.

One day, Michael's international got here crashing down. He had a setback, a public failure that shattered his self-photo and uncovered the frailty of his remarkable veneer. Dejected and disillusioned, Michael retreated into isolation, wondering approximately his identification and reason.

But amidst the darkness, a spark of possibility arose. Michael stumbled located a ebook approximately self-reputation. He have a study approximately the liberating effect of embracing imperfection, of recognizing that imperfections aren't screw ups, however in reality part of the human revel in.

The message resonated deeply inner Michael's soul. He came to look his constant quest for perfection now not as a course to success, but as a jail of his layout. He started out to impeach his bad self-communicate, converting it with affirmations of self-compassion and popularity.

It wasn't an clean journey. Years of ingrained behaviors and ingrained varieties of idea had been not definitely broken. However, Michael persisted, steadily eroding the walls of his meticulous prison.

He determined out to like his shortcomings, recognizing them as superb facets of his identity. He determined out to cope with failure now not as a setback, however as an opportunity for growth and getting to know. He began out to discover pleasure in the easy things, the laughter of a friend, the splendor of a sundown, the warmth of an include.

As Michael embraced his shortcomings, his existence began out out to transform. He grew greater calm, extra gift, and extra open to new reports. He made deeper ties with others, not judging or fearing their imperfections. He found a revel in of calm and contentment he had never known earlier than.

Michael's tale is a tribute to the transformative energy of self-splendor. It teaches us that:

Striving for perfection is a recipe for unhappiness. It results in persistent tension, worry, and a sensation of in no manner being correct enough.

Embracing our shortcomings is vital for self-love and recognition. When we receive ourselves, flaws and all, we will open ourselves as a good deal as a lifestyles of satisfaction and success.

Failure is a natural a part of lifestyles. It isn't always a mirrored photograph of our actually worth, but an possibility to take a look at and improvement.

The contemporary second is all we have. By specializing inside the present second and appreciating the small subjects, we are able to gain serenity and pleasure.

Life is a adventure, now not a vacation spot. It is ready analyzing, growing, and evolving. There may be usaand downs, but via accepting ourselves and embracing our shortcomings, we are capable of control the street with grace and resilience.

Michael's story is an notion to everybody who battles with perfectionism. It shows us that through the usage of embracing our shortcomings, we can also release the door to a happier, extra fulfilled existence.

Chapter 14: Cultivating Gratitude

Gratitude is an frequently-left out but effective tool for developing our nicely-being and resilience. It is the place of figuring out and appreciating the high-quality matters in our lives, whether or not or no longer awesome or small.

The Benefits of Gratitude:

Cultivating appreciation has been determined to have diverse advantages for our bodily and emotional nicely-being, which includes:

Increased happiness and well-being: People who exercise gratitude constantly report feeling happier, more positive, and greater satisfied with their lives.

Reduced strain and anxiety: Gratitude allows to change our consciousness from horrific ideas to wonderful ones, that could decrease stress and tension ranges.

Improved sleep: Focusing at the notable subjects in advance than bed might help us relax and doze off faster, number one to better sleep satisfactory.

Better connections: Gratitude can assist us recognize the exceptional factors of the humans in our lives, essential to higher and additional worthwhile relationships.

Enhanced coping abilties: When we confront hard conditions, gratitude can help us focus on the high nice factors of our lives and hold a revel in of desire and optimism.

Cultivating Gratitude in Your Life:

Here are some techniques you can consist of appreciation into your every day lifestyles:

Keep a thankfulness mag: Every night time time, write down 3 stuff you are grateful for. This might be a few factor from a high-quality meal you professional to a considerate gesture from someone you adore.

Practice aware appreciation: Take a while every day to genuinely appreciate the beauty of the arena round you. This can be spending time in nature, paying attention to your chosen tune, or relishing a tremendous meal.

Express your manner to others: Take the time to thank the human beings to your existence for the topics they do for you, each massive and small.

Focus on the satisfactory, even within the direction of difficult instances: When confronted with limitations, try to find out some factor to be happy approximately, irrespective of the truth that it's miles a few problem tiny.

Challenge terrible mind: When you note yourself questioning terrible thoughts, try and recast them in a extraordinary mindset. To counteract horrible mind, try thinking a few element like "This is a terrible day," like "This day has been hard, however I am grateful for the wonderful matters which have befell."

Gratitude isn't always a magic bullet, however it's far a sturdy device that would dramatically decorate our lives. By imposing thankfulness practices into our everyday exercises, we are able to create better satisfaction, nicely-being, and resilience.

A Story of Thankfulness: Emily's Journey to Finding Joy in Unexpected Places

Emily has usually struggled to understand the effective in lifestyles. Her emphasis end up commonly fixated on the awful, the faults, the wasted opportunities. This negativity threw a heavy shadow over her existence, hiding the satisfaction that lay buried all spherical her.

Her days had been packed with complaints and feedback. She observed defects within the entirety and everybody, locating fault even within the maximum pleasant conditions. This pessimism not handiest harmed her happiness but moreover strained her connections with others.

One day, Emily stumbled upon a ebook approximately gratitude. As she study, a spark of interest flared internal her. Could focusing on the immoderate high-quality elements of her existence, even the reputedly trivial ones, in fact make a distinction?

Skeptical but fascinated, Emily determined to offer it a try. She commenced truly, preserving a gratitude magazine and scribbling down three subjects she turned into glad for every day. At first, it changed into tough. Her negativity had end up a deeply ingrained addiction, and locating effective things to recognition on felt abnormal.

But with every passing day, it have end up a touch less hard. Emily commenced to see the beauty in the not unusual - the light on her cheeks, the laughter of a toddler, the warm temperature of an encompass. She started out appreciating the clean gestures of kindness from others, the surprising presence, and the moments of serenity within the commotion.

As Emily developed gratitude, a implausible shift commenced to unfold. Her outlook steadily transformed from negativity to optimism. She began to look the area in a brand new manner, noting the abundance of pinnacle spherical her.

The negativity that had previously engulfed her existence commenced out to recede. The lightness of delight began to replace the burden of negativity. Laughter have come to be greater commonplace, her interactions with others strengthened, and a experience of contentment settled within her.

Emily's adventure to gratitude wasn't usually easy. There had been days at the same time as the negativity seeped once more in, tempting her to slip back into her vintage behaviors. But by means of reminding herself of the wonderful tendencies in her life, she come to be capable of resist the trap of pessimism and preserve onto the newfound pride.

Emily's tale is a testomony to the transformative energy of thankfulness. It teaches us that:

Gratitude is a selection. We have the selection to pay interest on the coolest or the terrible.

Gratitude is a workout. It receives easier the more we exercising it.

Gratitude transforms our notion. It lets us see the arena in a new light, one full of possibility and delight.

Gratitude generates happiness. When we popularity on the coolest in our lives, we actually experience happier.

Gratitude is contagious. When we speak manner to others, it now not handiest improves their day but additionally conjures up them to grow gratitude of their private life.

Emily's story reminds us that pleasure is not a few issue we need to hunt for, it's already there, ready to be placed. By training thankfulness, we can open our eyes to the beauty and wealth that surrounds us, and include the delight this is our birthright.

Building a Support System: Sharing the Weight with Others

Humans are social beings. We are harassed to hook up with people and gather significant relationships. These connections offer us love, useful aid, and a experience of belonging, all of which is probably critical for our nicely-being.

A sturdy beneficial useful resource system may be a large advantage in times of warfare. It can provide us with the emotional, practical, and on occasion even financial aid we need to conquer troubles, address stress, and control existence's inevitable united statesand downs.

The Benefits of a Strong Support System:

Reduced strain and tension: Sharing our problems with others can assist in lowering tension and anxiety tiers. Talking about our problems may also permit us to advantage mind-set and create coping techniques.

Improved intellectual health: Strong social relationships have been confirmed to lessen the possibilities of despair and tension. Having people who care approximately us and help us can assist in growing our happiness and vanity.

Increased resilience: When we confront issues, a extraordinary assist tool can permit us to get higher faster and more potent. Knowing that we've were given individuals who consider in us and are there for us would possibly deliver us the power to undergo adversity.

Greater feeling of motive and belonging: Feeling associated with others can deliver us a enjoy of cause and belonging. Knowing that we're part of some thing bigger than ourselves can help in assuaging feelings of loneliness and isolation.

Enhanced bodily health: Research has confirmed that robust social ties can bring about advanced physical fitness effects, collectively with a lower hazard of coronary heart ailment, stroke, and dementia.

Building Your Support System:

Here are a few suggestions for developing a robust help system:

Nurture contemporary-day relationships: Invest effort and time into your current relationships with pals, own family, and associates. Show them which you care about them and are there for them in their moment of need.

Expand your social circle: Step out of doors your consolation quarter and meet new people. Join clubs or groups that share your pursuits, supply some time, or take a class.

Be open and sincere: Don't be afraid to talk approximately your views, feelings, and testimonies with those you take transport of as authentic with. Vulnerability can expand connections and deepen relationships.

Seek professional help: If you are trying to create a sturdy help device or are encountering hard troubles, bear in thoughts obtaining expert help from a therapist or counselor.

Remember, growing a robust guide device takes time and art work. Be patient, nurture your connections, and do now not be afraid to ask for assist whilst you need it.

A Story of Strong Bonds: Mark's Path to Reliance and Community

Mark had commonly been a solitary man or woman. He preferred the consolation of his very very personal organisation to the uncertainty of social engagement. He carried a robust dread of rejection and vulnerability, which saved him isolated and on my own.

Despite his need for connection, Mark positioned himself locked in a loop of self-reliance and independence. He took at the load of the whole thing himself, refusing to anticipate others for manual or help. This independent streak, even as appealing to a few, got here at a fee.

Mark felt a persistent sensation of isolation and loneliness. He not noted the satisfaction of shared testimonies, the warmth of human connection, and the sensation of belonging to a few thing bigger than himself.

Mark made the selection to alternate in the destiny. He identified that his worry of dependence modified into maintaining him again from experiencing the real richness of life. He determined out that he had to learn to consider others and be given them into his existence.

He started out gently, taking little one steps within the route of vulnerability. He confided in a honest buddy, disclosing a personal problem for the primary time. The enjoy modified into liberating, and it opened the door to a deeper connection together together with his accomplice.

As Mark persevered to open himself up, he started to create a network of helping friends. He joined a neighborhood trekking agency, locating shared pursuits and companionship amongst fellow out of doors lovers. He volunteered at a community animal secure haven, reading the delight of assisting others and giving once more to his community.

With each step, Mark chipped away at his walls of self-reliance and solitude. He positioned to accept as authentic with others, to depend on their guide, and to experience the strength that comes from belonging to a community.

The transformation became exceptional. Mark have emerge as extra easygoing, open, and personable. He smiled greater frequently, engaged in deeper conversations, and cherished a renewed experience of belonging. He discovered that sharing his troubles with others did now not make him vulnerable, but instead, it allowed him to be more absolutely human.

Mark's path is a tribute to the transformative energy of reliance and network. It shows us that:

Humans are social creatures. We thrive on connection and belonging.

Fear of vulnerability can hold us lower once more. Learning to accept as proper with others and open ourselves up is crucial for growing hit connections.

Seeking help need to no longer advise vulnerable factor. It is an indication of power and self-consciousness.

Community brings help and strength. Surrounding yourself with top notch people can assist us triumph over troubles and gain our goals.

Life is richer with shared memories. Connecting with others and sharing our reviews generates recollections and strengthens ties that very last a whole life.

Mark's revel in teaches us that we are not intended to walk on my own. By starting ourselves as lots as dependency and network, we can unharness a world of pleasure, support, and belonging, improving our lives in strategies we in no manner imagined.

Chapter 15: The Roots Of Rejection

Understanding the Fear: What is Social Rejection?

Defining Social Rejection

As we begin to recognize the nuanced realm of social rejection, we want to recognize it as an complicated and multifaceted phenomenon. At the leading edge of unraveling the ones complexities stands Elayne Savage, a luminary in information the nuances of rejection. With her clever insights, Savage has illuminated the mental underpinnings of rejection in her seminal paintings, Don't Take It Personally: The Art of Dealing with Rejection. Her contribution is big because it transcends the mere acknowledgment of rejection's pain, supplying a roadmap to navigate this hard emotional terrain. Through her knowledge, she aids in demystifying the fears and anxieties that rejection regularly breeds, equipping us with the system to cope and thrive in the face of such reviews. Her paintings resonates deeply with each person who has felt the threshold of being became away, making it a useful useful resource for expertise and overcoming the frequently-paralyzing fear of rejection. Savage, in her insightful explorations, reminds us that rejection isn't always genuinely a black-and-white state of affairs of being omitted or excluded through manner of buddies. The spectrum for which rejection is consists of greater subtle office work, frequently left out but in addition impactful. These diffused workplace work, which embody indifference or a lack of recognition, can insidiously erode our experience of belonging and self esteem. Savage poignantly notes, "Rejection may be seen as a dismissal of our sincerely worth, a discounting of our charge, or a discrediting of our aspirations." (2016)

The perceived or real elimination from social connection or reputation is at the coronary coronary coronary heart of social rejection. This revel in actions a chord deep internal our primal instincts. As people, we're hardwired for connection; our brains are sculpted by using way of evolution to are searching for and preserve social bonds. When these bonds are threatened or severed, it triggers a cascade of mental and emotional responses. This final results is not certainly a social inconvenience however a profound denial of our inherent want for belonging. Rejection, in its essence, is a denial of our social life. It whispers to our innermost selves that we are not enough, and our presence isn't always valued. Whether it's being unnoticed in a conversation, left out in a social placing, or explicitly excluded from a set, each example of rejection sends a effective message. This message, frequently internalized, can form our self-notion and our worldview.

The complexity of social rejection is similarly amplified thru manner of its subjective nature. What constitutes rejection for one character might not hold the identical which means for a few unique. This subjectivity underscores the importance of information rejection now not really as an external occasion however furthermore as an inner revel in. It is the internalization of rejection, the narrative we assemble spherical it, that often holds the maximum energy over us. In grasping the real breadth of social rejection, we start to see it as greater than simply an occasional unpleasant revel in. It turns into a large hassle in our mental panorama, a stress that might shape our conduct, our relationships, and our arrogance. By facts its many bureaucracy and the profound effect it can have, we take the first step closer to constructing resilience and redefining our dating with rejection.

The Spectrum of Rejection Experiences

In its myriad paperwork, rejection paints a spectrum that touches each thing of human interplay. From a easy snub at a celebration to profound ostracism in network or administrative center settings, each example of rejection resonates deeply inner us, irrespective of its apparent importance. Savage, in her illuminating artwork, captures this essence via declaring, "Even small rejections can sting because of the fact they generally echo in advance, more painful dismissals" (2016)

This spectrum of rejection opinions is essential to apprehend because of the reality its effect is cumulative. A seemingly insignificant incident of rejection, like at the same time as we're unnoticed in a set communique, may not seem impactful on its personal. Yet, the ones minor episodes can building up over the years, developing an undercurrent of emotional and mental distress. This accumulation effect is similar to how small, repetitive stresses can weaken a form over time, sooner or later main to cracks in its foundation.

On the greater intense give up of the spectrum, opinions collectively with bullying, ostracism, or betrayal in close to relationships convey a proper away and effective emotional fee. These kinds of rejection no longer simplest inflict right away pain but can also have lengthy-lasting consequences on our mental health, shaping our future interactions and perceptions of self esteem. Savage aptly notes, "The pain of rejection frequently lingers lengthy past the actual event, reinforcing self-doubt and creating a narrative of private failure" (2016)

Understanding this spectrum is important as it traumatic conditions us to redefine our belief of rejection. It isn't honestly the overt, unmistakable incidents that count number range however furthermore the subtle, often not noted ones. Recognizing the total kind of rejection lets in us to peer how they together have an impact on our emotional properly-being. It enables us understand why first-rate conditions cause disproportionate emotional responses - they are not truly reactions to the existing 2nd but echoes of beyond testimonies.

This interest invites us to approach our reviews with rejection with a cutting-edge lens, one which recognizes every their variety and cumulative impact. As we discover ways to find out and process those various reports, we empower ourselves to heal from past hurts and assemble resilience in opposition to destiny ones. Understanding the overall spectrum of rejection isn't quite an awful lot acknowledging ache; it's approximately recognizing the opportunity for boom and transformation that lies inner every experience, regardless of how small or reputedly insignificant.

The Psychological Impact of Being Rejected

Immediate Emotional Responses to Rejection

In the immediately aftermath of rejection, our emotional landscape frequently will become a tumultuous sea, with waves of harm, anger, disappointment, and confusion crashing over us. This surge of feelings, as Savage articulates, "presentations the primal pain deep indoors us, added on through manner of the perceived danger to our social belonging" (2016). These immoderate emotional responses aren't truly fleeting reactions but are deeply rooted in our mind's interpretation of rejection. Our brain perceives rejection as a giant hazard to our social status and, via extension, our experience of self. This stop result is a primal response etched into our evolutionary blueprint historically, being part of a group come to be synonymous with survival. Exclusion from the agency didn't just suggest social ache; it regularly spelled peril. This evolutionary context permits offer an cause in the back of why rejection triggers such profound emotional upheaval. It is not truly a contemporary-day social pain however a reason that echoes our ancestral fears.

The immediacy and depth of those emotional responses may be startling. They regularly come uninvited, sweeping over us with a pressure which can experience overwhelming. Savage aptly notes, "The immediacy with which those feelings floor elements to their deep roots in our psyche, a testomony to the vital position social belonging has played in our evolutionary statistics" (2016). This consciousness offers a crucial belief into the individual of rejection: it's miles more than a social setback; it's a profound mental occasion. Recognizing the primal origins of these emotional responses to rejection is critical to records their power and incidence. It moreover offers a pathway to coping with them more correctly. By acknowledging that those feelings are a natural, deeply ingrained reaction to perceived social threats, we will begin to approach them with more compassion and know-how.

Long-Term Psychological Effects

The lengthy-time period intellectual consequences of repeated rejection amplify some distance beyond the instantaneous emotional responses. As Savage observes, "The echo of repeated rejections can reverberate through our psyche, major to pervasive emotions of faded self confidence and an altered view of the arena" (2016]). These echoes can display up as reduced conceitedness, heightened anxiety or depression, and a modern sense of alienation from others.

Over time, those mental consequences can profoundly adjust our notion of the sector and our vicinity indoors it. This shift in belief frequently leads to a self-pleasant prophecy, in which the priority of rejection turns into a routine subject matter in our lives. We might usually anticipate rejection, that could affect our behaviors and interactions, potentially main to greater rejection. This cycle may be specifically insidious because it reinforces the fears and beliefs that power it.

The impact of persistent rejection is not great a quick emotional u . S . However a restructuring of our inner narrative. "Our memories with rejection, specifically whilst repetitive and unresolved, can bring about deeply ingrained ideals about our worthiness and belonging" (Savage, 2016]). These beliefs can form everything from interpersonal relationships to profession options, often restricting our capability and constricting our life studies.

Recognizing the prolonged-term outcomes of rejection is essential for breaking this cycle. It entails healing from past rejections and reshaping the narratives we've built spherical our self confidence and social belonging. This tool of healing and narrative reshaping is wherein we delve deeper into the roots of rejection fear, exploring its origins and impacts.

The Roots of Rejection Fear: A Deeper Dive

Early Life Experiences and Their Role

As we transition from knowledge rejection's at once and long-time period intellectual impacts, we delve into the pivotal feature of youth evaluations in shaping our belief and reaction to rejection Childhood, a critical length of emotional and mental development, devices the degree for navigating social dynamics throughout our lives. Savage's artwork gives profound insights into this component. She emphasizes, "Our earliest reviews of recognition or rejection within the own family and peer institution set a pattern for the way we recognize ourselves and react to new conditions" (2016). These early interactions, whether nurturing or neglectful, play a essential function in forming our self-photograph and expectancies of others and create the backdrop in competition to which our man or woman reminiscences of rejection play out.